Structure and Dynamics of the U.S. Federal Services Industrial Base, 2000–2012

Project Directors
David J. Berteau
Guy Ben-Ari

Lead Authors
Gregory Sanders
Jesse Ellman

Contributing Authors
Rhys McCormick
Andysheh Dadsetan

A Report of the CSIS Defense-Industrial Initiatives Group

September 2013

CSIS | CENTER FOR STRATEGIC & INTERNATIONAL STUDIES

ROWMAN & LITTLEFIELD
Lanham • Boulder • New York • Toronto • Plymouth, UK

About CSIS—50th Anniversary Year

For 50 years, the Center for Strategic and International Studies (CSIS) has developed solutions to the world's greatest policy challenges. As we celebrate this milestone, CSIS scholars are developing strategic insights and bipartisan policy solutions to help decisionmakers chart a course toward a better world.

CSIS is a nonprofit organization headquartered in Washington, D.C. The Center's 220 full-time staff and large network of affiliated scholars conduct research and analysis and develop policy initiatives that look into the future and anticipate change.

Founded at the height of the Cold War by David M. Abshire and Admiral Arleigh Burke, CSIS was dedicated to finding ways to sustain American prominence and prosperity as a force for good in the world. Since 1962, CSIS has become one of the world's preeminent international institutions focused on defense and security; regional stability; and transnational challenges ranging from energy and climate to global health and economic integration.

Former U.S. senator Sam Nunn has chaired the CSIS Board of Trustees since 1999. Former deputy secretary of defense John J. Hamre became the Center's president and chief executive officer in April 2000.

CSIS does not take specific policy positions; accordingly, all views expressed herein should be understood to be solely those of the author(s)

ISBN: 978-1-4422-2527-5 (pb); 978-1-4422-2528-2 (eBook)

Center for Strategic & International Studies
1800 K Street, NW, Washington, DC 20006
202-887-0200 | www.csis.org

Rowman & Littlefield
4501 Forbes Boulevard, Lanham, MD 20706
301-459-3366 | www.rowman.com

Table of Contents

List of Figures

List of Tables

Acknowledgments

The project on the Federal Services Industrial Base, now in its fifth edition, was initiated at CSIS in 2005. This report is dedicated to our friend, colleague, and mentor Guy Ben-Ari. He has guided this report, and those that work on it, since its inception, and the principles he embodied will direct it going forth.

Among our colleagues at the Center for Strategic and International Studies, we would like to thank Joshua Archer, Sneha Raghavan, Tomoyo Nishimori, and Luke Heselden for their considerable assistance in preparing the data used in this series of studies. The authors would also like to thank the numerous individuals who have supported the project since then: Stan Soloway, Alan Chvotkin, and Roger Jordan of the Professional Services Council, for their insights into the dynamics of the federal services industry, and Bradley Nelson of the Defense Department's Office of Industrial Policy for his insights into defense contract data. Finally, we would like to thank all those in government that have answered our questions and whose hard work and dedication make this research possible.

Executive Summary

The U.S. government has a permanent reliance on contracts with the private sector for a wide range of services, though the share of federal services contracts has declined slightly in recent years. For the past eight years, the Defense-Industrial Initiatives Group (DIIG) at the Center for Strategic and International Studies (CSIS) has tracked the trends driving the services industry. Overall, this report analyzes the trends for all federal services contract obligations from FY 2000 through FY 2012, the most recent full fiscal year for which reliable data are available from the Federal Procurement Data System (FPDS). This Executive Summary provides an overall view of the data and trends, including projections for federal services contract spending over the next 3 years (FY 2013–2015).[1, 2]

The chart to the right shows actual and projected totals for federal discretionary outlays and services contract obligations, with projections both with and without the effects of sequestration. Using Congressional Budget Office (CBO) budget forecasts, CSIS projects that, by 2015, federal service contract obligations will still be below the level of 2009. If projected budgets drop in 2014 and 2015, then federal service contract obligations may also fall, in real dollar terms, to levels not seen since the middle of the previous decade.

The decline in federal services contracting had already begun to show in the FY 2010 data of our prior report.[3] The share of total federal discretionary outlays going to services contract obligations fell from 27 percent in 2009 to 25 percent in 2010, and declined further to 24 percent in 2011. The decline between 2010 and 2011 is partially due to a reduced impact from the American Recovery & Reinvestment Act (ARRA) of 2009, which had temporarily increased services contract obligations in 2009 and 2010. As Chapter 5 of the report discusses, ARRA-related services accounted for 5 percent of overall federal services contract obligations in those years.

Federal Discretionary Outlays and Services Contract Obligations, with Projection Based on Budget Forecasts

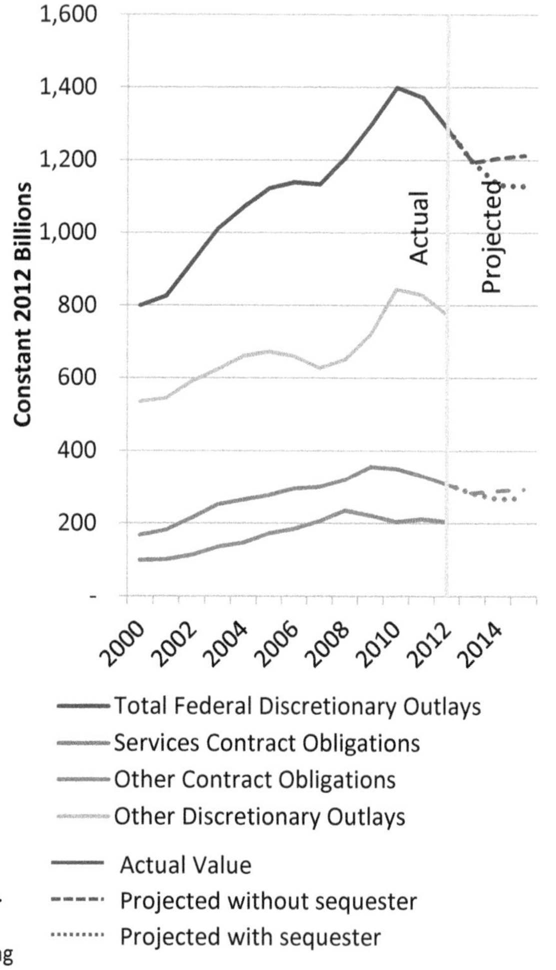

[1] To account for the effects of inflation, all dollar figures, with the exception of thresholds used to judge contract size, are in 2012 dollars.
[2] The CSIS projection in the above figure was extrapolated from 2000–2012 real federal discretionary spending and percentage spending on federal services contract obligations. Historical budget figures came from the Office of Management and Budget. CBO budget projections for 2013–2015 include overseas contingency operations funding. An ARIMA (autoregressive integrated moving average) model was used, correcting for first-order autocorrelation.
[3] See Gregory Sanders, David Morrow, and Jesse Ellman, *Structure and Dynamics of the U.S. Federal Services Industrial Base 2000–2010* (Washington, DC: CSIS, November 2011), http://csis.org/files/publication/111123_Services_2011.pdf.

The decline since 2010 has been larger than just a reduction in ARRA spending, but the rate of decline in services contract obligations slowed in the last year. Between 2011 and 2012, as total federal discretionary outlays declined by 6 percent, overall federal services contract obligations declined by 7 percent, from $331.5 billion in 2011 to $307.8 billion in 2012. As a share of overall federal discretionary outlays, however, federal services contract obligations declined from 24.2 percent to 23.9 percent between 2011 and 2012, a drop one-third as steep as between 2010 and 2012. Compared to other contracts, since 2009, federal services contract obligations have declined, at nearly twice the rate (-4.7 percent 3-year compound annual growth rate, CAGR) of non-service federal contract obligations (-2.6 percent 3-year CAGR).

This summary now looks at federal services contracting trends in competition, contract funding mechanisms, contract vehicles, and contract size.

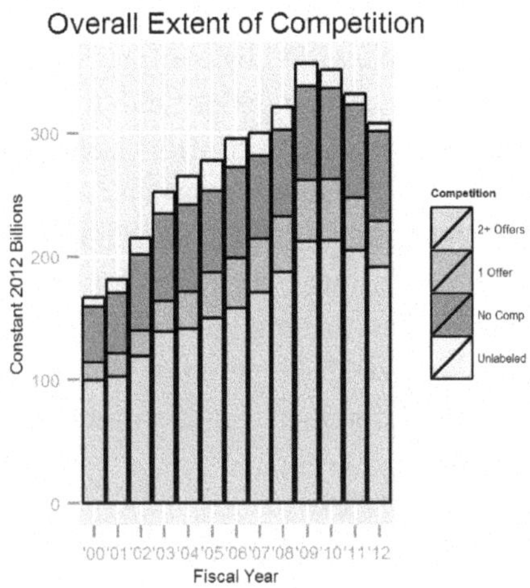

Competition

Sixty-two percent of federal services contract obligations were awarded under the category of "Competition with Multiple Offers" in both 2011 and 2012, the highest share since at least 2000. Within that category, however, "Limited Competition with Multiple Offers" has accounted for a growing share, consistent with the rise of multiple-award indefinite delivery contracts (IDCs) in federal services contracting. As discussed in the Policy Implications section below, agencies appear to be receiving the benefits of competition under multiple-award IDCs. Competed contract obligations receiving only a single offer declined from 13 percent of overall services contract obligations in 2011 to 12 percent in 2012. This change shows the potential for further increases in effective competition via policy attention toward determining why these competed contract actions receive only a single offer.

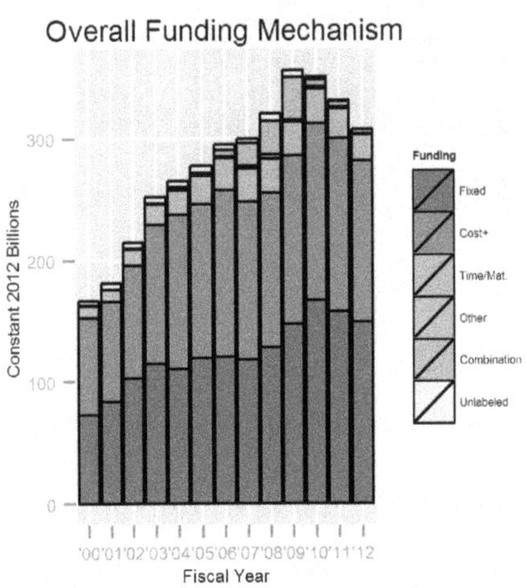

Contract Funding Mechanisms

The share of services contract obligations awarded under fixed price contracts rose from 48 percent in 2011 to 49 percent in 2012, while the share awarded under cost reimbursement contracts held steady at 43 percent. Despite federal government-wide guidance to increase the use of fixed-price contracts, it appears that there have been only marginal increases in their usage for services contracts. Further, it appears that the minimal increases have been primarily the result of better labeling of "Combination" contracts, rather than any actual increase in the use of fixed-price contracts.

Contract Vehicles

The biggest story told by the data on contract vehicles used in federal services contracting is the rise of multiple-award IDCs, which have grown from 6 percent of services contract obligations in 2000 to 20 percent in 2012. That growth has continued even during the current budget downturn (2.4 percent 3-year CAGR), as the only contract vehicle type to show growth from 2009–2012. The policy implications section of this report (Chapter 5) expands on the rise of multiple-award IDCs in federal services contracting. The category of "Definitive Contracts" (45 percent in 2011, 46 percent in 2012) still account for the largest share of services contract obligations, while the category of "Single-Award IDCs" (23 percent in 2011, 22 percent in 2012) remains a significant factor in federal services contracting.

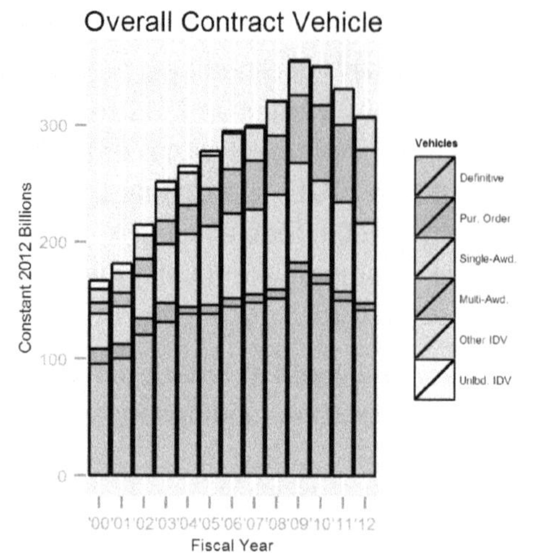

Contract Size

Looking at services contract obligations by size of contract (classified by contract value awarded in the given year), the most notable trend has been the dramatic decline in contract obligations for smaller contracts, those for less than $250,000 in a given year. Contract obligations for such contracts have been cut in half since 2010, from $16.0 billion to $7.7 billion. Contract obligations for contracts in the range of $25–$100 million and of greater than $500 million both declined at a slower rate (-3 percent) than did overall services contract obligations between 2011 and 2012 (-7 percent). The remaining contract size categories saw declines roughly in line with the overall -7 percent decline in services contract obligations between 2011 and 2012.

Service Areas

CSIS separates services contracts into six categories: information and communications technology (ICT); professional, administrative, and management support (PAMS); research and development (R&D); equipment-related services (ERS); facilities-related services and construction (FRS&C); and medical services (MED). Chapter 3 of this report looks at trends for each of them in turn. Comparing 2011 and 2012, most service areas declined by -7 to -8 percent, roughly in sync with the overall decline in federal services contract obligations. One service area, ERS, saw a rise in contract obligations, expanding from $29.3 billion to $31 billion, a 7 percent increase. A second service area, FRS&C, declined more steeply (-11 percent).

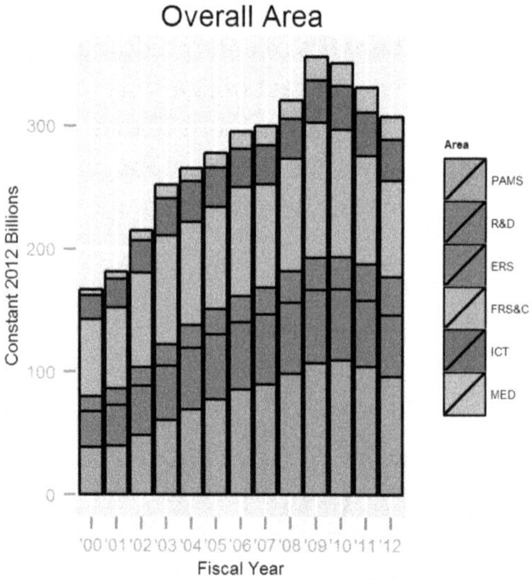

ICT (Information and Communications Technology)

Overall ICT contract obligations peaked in 2011 before falling by more than $2 billion (6 percent) between 2011 and 2012. The Department of Defense (DoD), which accounts for half of ICT contract obligations, accounted for most of this. The Big 6 vendors (Boeing, Lockheed Martin, Northrop Grumman, General Dynamics, Raytheon, and BAE) saw a faster decline than overall ICT.

PAMS (Professional, Administrative, and Management Support)

PAMS contract obligations peaked in 2010 at near $110 billion, but then declined by more than $13 billion by 2012, partly in response to OMB guidance for agencies to reduce contract obligations for management support. Within PAMS, contract obligations awarded under fixed price (41 percent in 2010,

47 percent in 2012) have gained ground versus cost reimbursement (40 percent in 2010, 47 percent in 2012). Contract obligations awarded under single-award IDCs have declined sharply (-10.3 percent 3-year CAGR) from 2009–2012.

R&D (Research and Development)

Overall R&D contract obligations declined by over $10 billion from their 2009 peak, with a drop of nearly $5 billion from 2011 to 2012. Contract obligations awarded to the Big 6 vendors have declined steeply (-11.0 percent 3-year CAGR), falling as a share of overall R&D from 49 percent in 2009 to 42 percent in 2012.

ERS (Equipment-Related Services)

The only service area to grow from 2009 to 2012, ERS gained more than $5 billion during that period, a 6.4 percent 3-year CAGR. DoD, which accounted for over 85 percent of contract obligations, saw growth in line with overall ERS (5.8 percent 3-year CAGR) between 2009 and 2012.

FRS&C (Facilities-Related Services and Construction)

Overall FRS&C contract obligations declined by well over $13 billion from their 2009 peak of over $109 billion, though 2009 and 2010 figures were temporarily inflated by the American Recovery & Reinvestment Act of 2009. Contract obligations fell by 11 percent between 2011 and 2012, in large part due to a GSA reporting change discussed below in the GSA section. Contract obligations awarded to the Big 6 vendors saw slight growth (1.7 percent 3-year CAGR) even as overall FRS&C declined.

MED (Medical Services)

Overall medical services (MED) contract obligations peaked in 2011 at $9.8 billion, but even after a 7 percent decline between 2011 and 2012, obligations were still higher than any fiscal year from 2000–2010. DoD, which accounted for over 70 percent of MED contract obligations, saw only a 3 percent decline between 2011 and 2012.

Government Agency

Overall federal services contract obligations have been in decline since 2009, but this has not affected all government agencies equally. The Department of Homeland Security (DHS) initially peaked in 2006, but experienced a smaller peak in 2009 before dropping off. The Departments of Defense, Energy (DoE), and State/USAID all peaked in 2009. NASA, the Government Services Administration (GSA), and other agencies peaked in 2010. Health and Human Services (HHS) had peaked in 2010, but its 2012 value represents an increase over 2011 and 2009. Here are some additional details on key government agency users of service contracts.

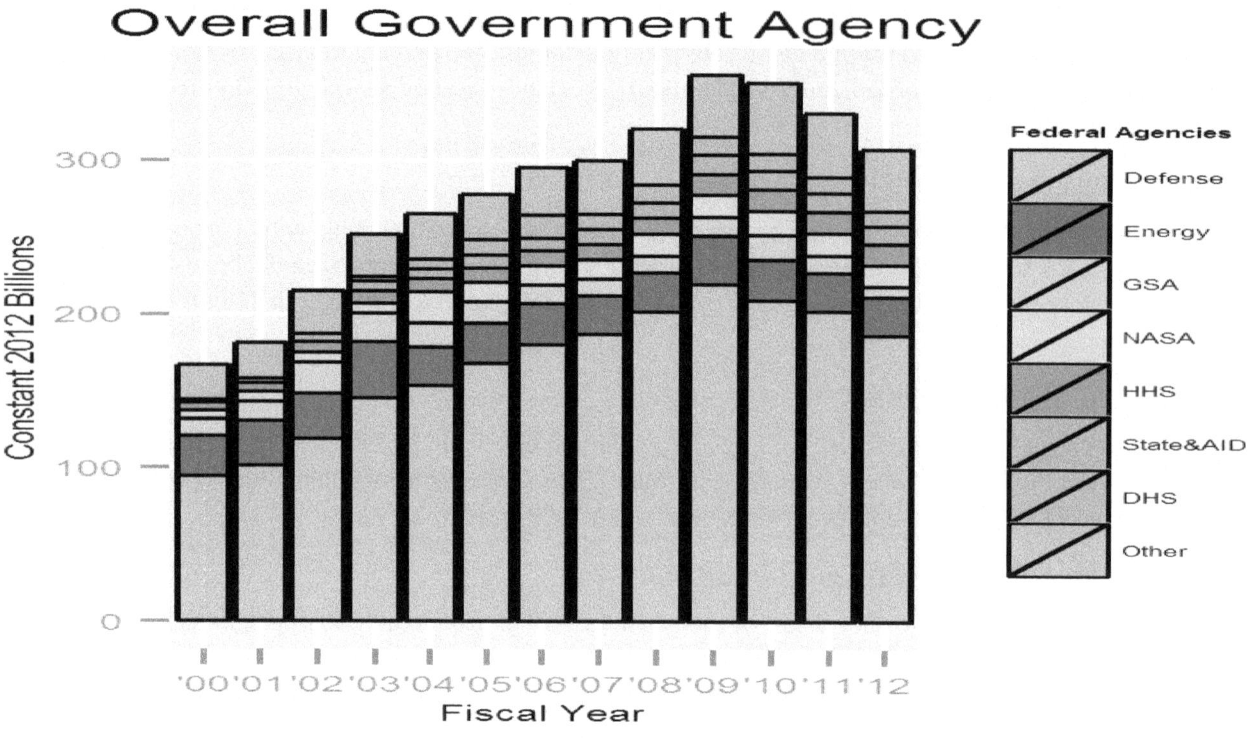

DoD

Overall DoD services contract obligations declined by nearly $33 billion from 2009 to 2012, with more than $15 billion of that decline between 2011 and 2012. ERS saw moderate growth despite the overall decline (5.8 percent 3-year CAGR), while FRS&C declined sharply (-11.4 percent 3-year CAGR). Contract obligations awarded under multiple-award IDCs (1.2 percent 3-year CAGR) and Federal Supply Schedule (FSS) and other indefinite delivery vehicles (IDVs) (8.1 percent 3-year CAGR) grew even as overall DoD services contracting declined.

DHS

DHS has seen dramatic increases in the shares of contract obligations awarded after competition with multiple offers (from 38 percent in 2009 to 57 percent in 2012) and awarded under fixed price contract types (from 43 percent of contract obligations in 2009 to 54 percent in 2012).Overall DHS services contract obligations declined by $2 billion from 2009 to 2012, steadily falling at a -6 percent 3-year CAGR. Contract obligations for PAMS also fell by $2 billion (-13.3 percent 3-year CAGR). Unlike for most other government agencies, contract obligations awarded under multiple-award IDCs declined sharply (-13.3 percent 3-year CAGR), from 49 percent of contract obligations in 2009 to 38 percent in 2012.

DoE

Overall DoE services contract obligations declined by more than $7 billion from 2009–2012, with more than $6 billion of that decline between 2009 and 2010 due to the temporary ARRA-related obligations in 2009. R&D contract obligations held steady (0.2 percent 3-year CAGR) even as overall R&D declined. From 2009 to 2012, 75 percent of DoE contract obligations were awarded after competition with multiple offers. Almost all DoE services contract obligations are awarded under fixed price contract types and under definitive contracts (over 95 percent for both.)

HHS

HHS was the only government agency to see service contract obligations increase (2 percent) from 2011 to 2012. The department has fluctuated above $13 billion since 2009, with a 2012 total of $13.8 billion, only slightly below its prior peak of $14 billion in 2010. ICT contract obligations grew strongly (11.9 percent 3-year CAGR), while R&D contract obligations declined sharply (-10.7 percent 3-year CAGR).

GSA

Analysis of GSA services contracting trends is distorted, due to GSA no longer reporting approximately $4.7 billion of contract obligations for lease of office buildings (which falls under FRS&C) into FPDS, a figure that would represent 39 percent of GSA's services contracting inventory if carried forward into 2012. Although there is no clear public statement of a policy reason for this change, it is discussed in more detail in the GSA section of Chapter 4. Overall GSA services contract obligations declined by nearly $9 billion since the 2010 peak, with more than $4 billion of that drop between 2011 and 2012, a 36 percent drop.

NASA

Overall NASA services contract obligations peaked above $15 billion in 2010 and dropped off to $14 billion in 2012. Contract obligations awarded for PAMS have dropped significantly (-11.6 percent 3-year CAGR), while contract obligations for R&D rose (3.1 percent 3-year CAGR).

State & USAID

Overall State/USAID services contract obligations declined by over $1 billion since 2009, with $800 million of that decline from 2011 to 2012. That decline still left State/USAID with well over $11 billion in obligations, more than any year prior to 2009. Over half of State/USAID services contract obligations were still awarded for PAMS from 2009 to 2012.

Industrial Base

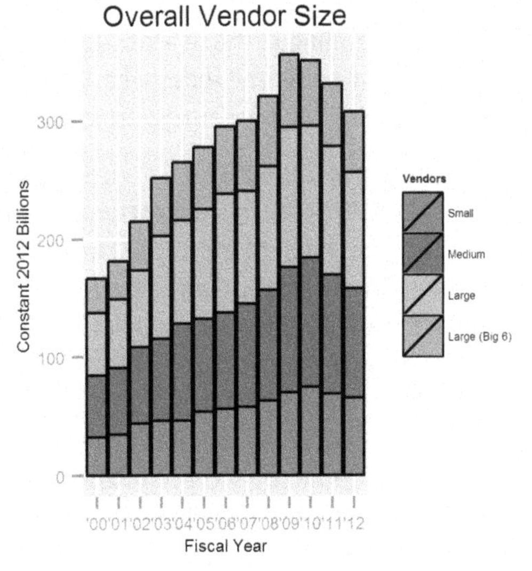

In recent years, small vendors (as designated by FPDS, with some adjustment, as described in the methodology) accounted for around 20 percent of federal services contract obligations. Medium vendors (any vendor with overall annual revenue from all sources of less than $3 billion that is not 'small') and large vendors (defined as having overall annual revenue, from all sources, above $3 billion) have both consistently accounted for approximately 30 percent of federal services contract obligations. Separated from large, the Big 6 vendors (Boeing, Lockheed Martin, Northrop Grumman, General Dynamics, Raytheon, and BAE) have held a steady share of overall federal services contract obligations with percentages in the mid to high teens. Although services contract obligations awarded to the Big 6 (and to large vendors) have declined slightly faster than overall service contract obligations between 2009 and 2012, those declines were frontloaded. Small vendors and medium vendors peaked in 2010, and their rates of decline from 2011 to 2012 were twice that of 2009 to 2012.

The report looks at the impact of contract vehicles on small and medium vendors. In this report, the study team analyzed the 2012 data in detail. Medium vendors held roughly equivalent shares (around 30 percent) of services contract obligations awarded under definitive contracts, single-award IDCs, and multiple-award IDCs. Large vendors accounted for a proportionally lower share of services contract obligations awarded under single-award IDCs (26 percent) than other prominent contract vehicles, while the Big 6 vendors accounted for a relatively small share (12 percent) of services contract obligations awarded under multiple-award IDCs. See Chapter 5 for further discussion of the implications of these findings.

The report also looks at the connection between annual contract obligations and vendor size. Data for 2012 show that it is hard for medium and small vendors to win larger services contracts. Small vendors reach their peak share on contracts with $1 million to $5 million in obligations. Medium vendors reach their peak share with contracts with annual obligations between $5 million and $25 million. Above $25 million, large vendors dominate, with the Big 6 growing in share with each larger category. See Chapter 5 for further discussion of the implications of these findings.

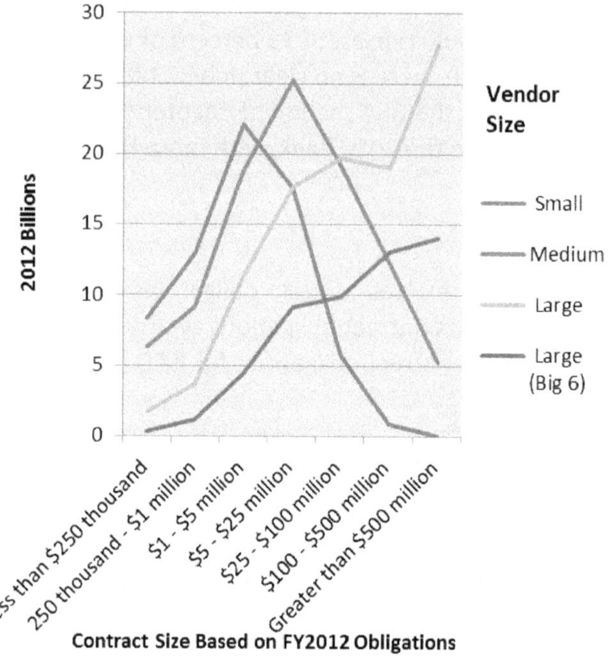

The top 20 federal services vendors in 2002 and 2012 (by total federal services contract obligations) were remarkably similar, with five of the top six largely unchanged: Lockheed Martin, Boeing, Northrop Grumman, Raytheon, and General Dynamics. The rest of the top 20 in 2012 show an increase in the number of IT and medical firms since 2002, reflecting the increased spending in those areas across the federal government. The top 5 services vendors accounted for 20 percent of overall federal services contract obligations in 2002, but only 16 percent in 2012. This trend of decreasing concentration suggests a broader base of services firms.

However, the top 20 services vendors remain heavily weighted to DoD between 2002 and 2012, and that concentration has grown in the past decade. DoD awarded 75 percent of services contract obligations awarded to the top 20 in 2012, compared to 58 percent in 2002. By contrast, looking at service area participation among the top 20, there has been significant deconcentration in the last decade. FRS&C contract obligations in the top 5 have dropped significantly, largely due to changes in contract awards for management of the national nuclear laboratories, but contract obligations in every other category except MED have increased significantly. It is notable that, unlike in 2002, every vendor in the top 5 in 2012 has been awarded over $1 billion in contract obligations in three or more service areas (compared to only three in 2002), showing the degree to which the biggest companies have diversified in order to maintain or increase their share of the federal services contracting market. Looking at trends for all services vendors across service areas, a growing percentage of services vendors are expanding into the PAMS market, and to a lesser degree into ERS and MED.

Policy Implications: Focus on Competition

The FY 2010 CSIS report on services contracts notes that the stalling after a decade of heady growth was not a temporary blip, and as projected above, this trend is likely to continue.

For this report, CSIS has updated our classification of competition to capture additional data on indefinite delivery vehicles, and to allow cross-walking with government competition data. Chapter 5 takes a closer look at the depth of competition for various contract vehicles. Notably, multiple-award contract obligations have the highest share of competition with three or more offers, but also a substantial share of multiple-award IDCs with single-offer competition.

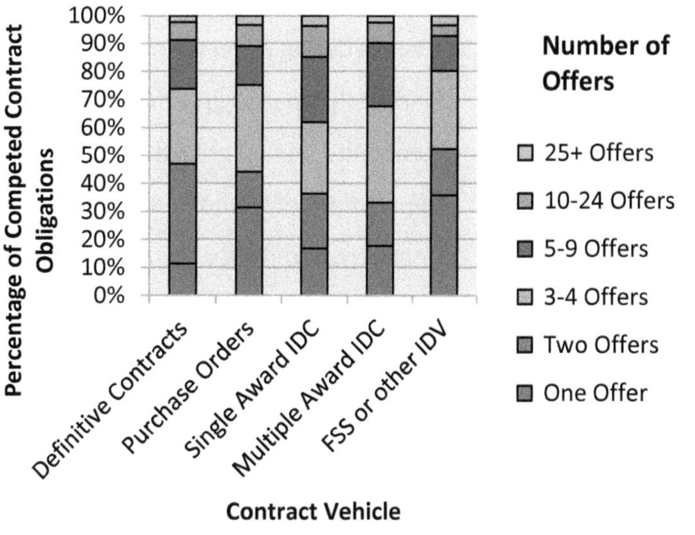

Definitive contracts have the lowest share of one-offer competition. However, they have the highest percentage of competitions with exactly two offers. This is driven by the size of many of the definitive contracts. Among services contracts with annual value over $500 million, 61 percent were awarded with only two offers, two to four times the rate of any other contract size category.

Overall, this report shows the beginning of a decline in federal services contracting that is largely commensurate with the declining overall federal budget and expenditure levels. It remains to be seen whether the FY 2013 levels, with the impact of sequestration under the Budget Control Act of 2011, will maintain that relationship or not. Next year's report will focus on the impacts of sequestration and additional budget reductions.

List of Acronyms

BOA	Basic Ordering Agreement
BPA	Blanket Purchase Agreement
CAGR	compound annual growth rate
DHS	Department of Homeland Security
DoD	Department of Defense
DoE	Department of Energy
DoS	Department of State
ERS	equipment-related services
FAPIIS	Federal Awardee Performance and Integrity Information System
FPDS	Federal Procurement Data System
FPDS–NG	Federal Procurement Data System–Next Generation
FRS&C	facilities-related services and construction
FSC	federal supply classification
GAO	Government Accountability Office
GSA	General Services Administration
GWAC	Government-Wide Acquisitions Contract
HHS	Department of Health and Human Services
ICT	information and communications technology
IDC	indefinite delivery contract
IDIQ	indefinite delivery indefinite quantity
IDV	indefinite delivery vehicle
NASA	National Aeronautics and Space Administration
OFPP	Office of Federal Procurement Policy
OMB	Office of Management and Budget
PAMS	professional, administrative, and management support
PPIRS	Past Performance Information Retrieval System
R&D	Research and Development
VA	Department of Veterans Affairs
USAID	U.S. Agency for International Development

Chapter 1: Analyzing Federal Services Contracting

For the purpose of this study, the U.S. federal services industrial base is defined as all vendors and individuals that are awarded service contracts by U.S. federal government departments and agencies. Service contracts include all types of contracts, including research and development (R&D) contracts, except contracts that are directly for products, such as supplies, weapons, fuel, and other goods.

Methodology of the Study

Most of the data used for this study were derived from the Federal Procurement Data System (FPDS). This government database covers all federal contract actions that have been awarded during a particular year by approximately 70 executive branch agencies (the largest exceptions are the U.S. Postal Service, the Federal Aviation Administration, and the Central Intelligence Agency). Initially created in 1979 by the Department of Defense (DoD), the FPDS has been managed by the General Services Administration (GSA) since 1980. In 2004, the database was significantly restructured and renamed FPDS–Next Generation (FPDS-NG).

The CSIS study team analyzed all federal contracts awarded between the fiscal years 2000 and 2012. Unless otherwise noted, all references to years in this report refer to the fiscal year based on the federal calendar. Because of the limitations of the online FPDS database, the study team has traditionally built a series of annual databases to make the challenge of FPDS's sheer size manageable. This year, the team has upgraded its tools and created a single database with all 35 million rows of data and all of the data fields available through USAspending.gov. Product data still is excluded from this report, but as will be discussed below, having all the study period data across all years improves the quality of our services data.

To obtain a better degree of granularity when analyzing the data, the team chose six service categories to represent broad areas of service types. The categories were created with the federal supply classification (FSC) codes (also referred to as product or service codes, or PSCs). All services—including research and development work—are assigned by the federal government a four-digit code, sometimes referred to as an "A–Z Code," which identifies 24 main categories of services. The list of all 24 FPDS service categories can be found in the appendix.

The six categories created by the CSIS study team for this study are:

- **Information and communications technology (ICT) services:** All of service codes D (Automatic data processing and telecommunication services) and L (Technical representative services), and elements of service codes H (Quality control, testing, and inspection services), J (Maintenance, repair, and rebuilding of equipment), K (Modification of equipment), N (Installation of equipment), S (Utilities and housekeeping services), and W (Lease or rental of equipment).

- **Professional, administrative, management services (PAMS):** All of service codes B (Special studies and analyses (not research and development), C (Architect and engineering services—construction), R, T, and U (Education and training services), and elements of service codes A (Research and development), H (Quality control, testing, and inspection services), and V (Transportation, travel, and relocation services).

- **Research and development (R&D):** Basic and applied research, experimental and advanced development, engineering, and operational systems development. This area includes all contracts with FSC codes in category A (R&D), except those ending with the digit 6 (digit 6 represents R&D management and support services, which are included in the PAMS area).

- **Equipment-related services (ERS):** Elements of service codes J (Maintenance, repair, and rebuilding of equipment), K (Modification of equipment), N (Installation of equipment), P (Salvage services), V (Transportation, travel, and relocation services), and W (Lease or rental of equipment).
- **Facility-related services & construction (FRS&C) services**: All of service codes E (Purchase of structures and facilities), F (Natural resources management), M (Operation of government-owned facility), X (Lease or rental of facilities), Y (Construction of structures and facilities), and Z (Maintenance, repair, or alteration of real property), and elements of service codes S (Utilities and housekeeping services) and P (Salvage services).
- **Medical (MED) services:** All of service codes G (Social services) and Q (Medical services).

Inherent Restrictions of FPDS

Due to the fact that it relies almost exclusively on FPDS data, the analysis presented in this report incurs five notable restrictions. First, contracts awarded as part of supplemental packages are not separately classified in FPDS or this report. As a result, we do not distinguish between contracts funded by base budgets and those funded by supplemental appropriations. Second, FPDS includes only prime contracts, and, as is discussed in the Policy Implications chapter, the separate subcontract database is radically incomplete. Therefore, only prime contract data are included in this report. Third, reporting regulations only require that unclassified contracts be included in FPDS. We interpret this to mean that few, if any, classified contracts are in the database. For DoD, this omits a substantial amount of total contract spending, perhaps as much as 10 percent. Such omissions are probably most noticeable in R&D contracts. Finally, it should be noted that classifications of contracts differ between FPDS and individual vendors. For example, some contracts that a vendor may consider as services are labeled as products in FPDS, and vice versa. This may cause some discrepancies between vendors' reports and those of the federal government.

Constant Dollars and Fiscal Years

All dollar amounts in this report are reported as constant fiscal year 2012 dollars unless specifically noted otherwise. Dollar amounts for all years were deflated by the implicit GDP deflator calculated by the U.S. Bureau of Economic Analysis, with FY 2012 as the base year. This measurement allowed the CSIS team to more accurately compare and analyze changes in spending across time. Similarly, all compound annual growth values and percentage growth comparison are based on constant dollars and thus adjusted for inflation.

Similarly, due to the native format of FPDS and the ease of comparison with government databases, all references to years conform to the federal fiscal years. Thus fiscal year 2012, the most recent complete year in the database, spans October 1, 2011, to September 30, 2012.

Small, Medium, and Large Companies

To analyze the breakdown of competitors in the market into small, medium, and large companies, the CSIS team assigned each vendor in the database to one of these size categories. Any organization designated as small by the FPDS database—according to the criteria established by the federal government—was categorized as such unless the vendor was a known subsidiary of a larger entity. Note that an organization may be identified as small for one set of contract actions but not for another as it may meet the criteria for being a small business in certain contract actions and not in others. The study team did not override these inconsistent entries when calculating the distribution of value by vendor size.

Vendors with annual revenue of more than $3 billion are classified as large. This classification is made based on their most recent revenue figure at time of classification. For vendors that have gone out of business or been acquired, this date may be well before 2012. A joint venture between two or more organizations is treated as a single separate entity and those with a large parent were also defined as large.

To better analyze the companies in the federal services market, the study team made significant efforts to consolidate data related to subsidiary companies and merged companies with their parent companies. For example, while a company's subsidiaries and predecessor companies are listed separately in FPDS, they are combined into a single entry in the CSIS services database. The assignment of vendor revenue is done on an annual basis and a merger must be completed by the end of March to be consolidated for that given fiscal year. This enabled the study team to analyze more accurately the services industrial base, the number of players in it, and their level of activity.

Over the past four years, the study team applied a systematic approach to these vendor roll ups. Since the prior report, there have been significant changes in the raw data. FPDS still uses hundreds of thousands of DUNS codes from Dun and Bradstreet to identify service providers, but they have switched from detailed 13-digit codes to standardized 9-digit codes. A salutary benefit of that standardization is that FPDS now provides parent vendor codes. As mentioned above, since the previous report the team has also consolidated the FPDS data for the study period into a single database. These two changes have allowed us to undertake significant upgrades to the vendor parent assignments.

The study team had previously investigated and classified all DUNS numbers associated with more than $500 million of *services* contract revenue in any single year. Building off the work of our departmental reports, we have now expanded *and lowered* that criterion to $250 million of total product *and* service revenue. We have also added an alternate threshold and investigate every DUNS number with more than $1 billion in obligations between 2000 and 2012, no matter how much they receive in any individual year.

We have reinforced these manual DUNS number assignments with automated assignments based on the vendor name. We have used a variety of means to make these assignments, but they are all variations on a single theme. Qualifying for automated assignment by name requires three criteria: 1) a standardized vendor name matches with the name of a parent vendor, 2) that name has been matched to the parent vendor by CSIS or is matched by DUNS number according to Bloomberg Government or the Parent DUNS number field, and 3) there are no alternative CSIS assignments of that vendor name. This process is not immune to error, but it increases the consistency of our assignments across the entire study period, which reduces the risk that a DUNS number is considered large in one year but overlooked in another.

Building on and double-checking the prior two steps, the study team compares our assignments to those made by Parent DUNS number for every DUNS number with $500 million in annual obligations or $2 billion in total obligations, and investigates contradictions. These discrepancies must be manually investigated because Parent DUNS number assignments, like Bloomberg Government assignments, are not backward looking. There are no separate records for back years, and thus a merger that happened in 2010 would affect parent assignments in 2000. By contrast, vendor names and DUNS numbers are accurate at the time of assignment, and thus we are comfortable in using those methods for automatic assignments.

Finally, to identify large vendors, the study team investigates any vendor with total obligations of $500 million in a single year or $2 billion over the study period. Determining revenues is the most labor-intensive part of the process and involves use of vendor websites, news articles, various databases, and public financial documents. All of this work taken together explains the increase in the market share of large vendors versus our prior report. While large vendors are, on rare occasions, reassigned into the middle tier, the vast majority of investigations either maintain the status quo or identify small or medium vendors that should be classified as large.

New and Modified Tables and Figures

With the exception of the data improvements and adjustments to new product or service codes mentioned above, the core figures of the report remain largely unchanged. There are two notable exceptions: contract vehicles and level of competition.

The change to contract vehicles is predominantly behind the scenes. In previous reports, the study team relied on separate queries using the FPDS web tool to gain access to the referenced indefinite delivery vehicle (IDV) fields to classify contract vehicles. Those fields are still unavailable from USAspending.gov, but thanks to our technical upgrades, the study team was able to largely reconstruct them. This switch allows cross-tabulation discussed below and removes the discrepancies that result from use of multiple sources.

Another benefit of reconstructing vehicle information is that it allows us to apply Department of Defense (DoD) methodology for classifying competition. Under current DoD methods, certain indefinite delivery contracts (IDCs) are classified using a different field that is focused on competitions after the initial offering. This change both makes this report more closely comparable to DoD reporting and better reflects the level of competition in these increasingly prevalent contract vehicles.

The study team has introduced several new figures to the policy implication chapter. These figures cross-tabulate the data on contract characteristics, specifically: multiple-award IDCs, contract size, vendor size, and competition. In addition, there is analysis exploring how the temporary stimulus of the American Recovery and Reinvestment Act of 2009 affected trends in recent years.

Data Reliability Notes and Download Dates

Any analysis based on the FPDS is naturally limited by the quality of the underlying data. Several Government Accountability Office (GAO) studies have highlighted the problems of FPDS (for example, the December 30, 2003, report: "Reliability of Federal Procurement Data," and the September 27, 2005, report: "Improvements Needed for the Federal Procurement Data System–Next Generation").

In addition, the FPDS data for past years is constantly updated over time. While fiscal year 2007 was long closed, over $100 billion worth of entries for that year were modified in 2010. This explains the discrepancies between the data presented in this report and those in previous editions. Such changes to FPDS may well be worthwhile, but should be monitored and clearly identified due to the potential for misunderstanding and abuse.

Yet despite its flaws, FPDS is the only comprehensive data source of government contracting activity and is more than adequate for any analysis that is focused on trends and order-of-magnitude comparisons.[4] In order to be transparent about weaknesses in the data, this report consistently describes data that could not be classified due to missing fields as "unlabeled" rather than including them in an "other" category.

The 2012 data used in this report was downloaded in February of 2013. The 2000–2011 data were downloaded between September and December 2012. In addition, the online FPDS query tool (available at https://www.fpds.gov) was used in May 2013 to generate data for on the ARRA discussed in chapter 5.

---

[4] See Chapter 5 for recommendations on improving FPDS.

Chapter 2: Overall Federal Services Contracting Trends

Top Line Federal Contract Obligations and Outlays

Figure 2-1: Top Line Federal Contract Obligations and Outlays

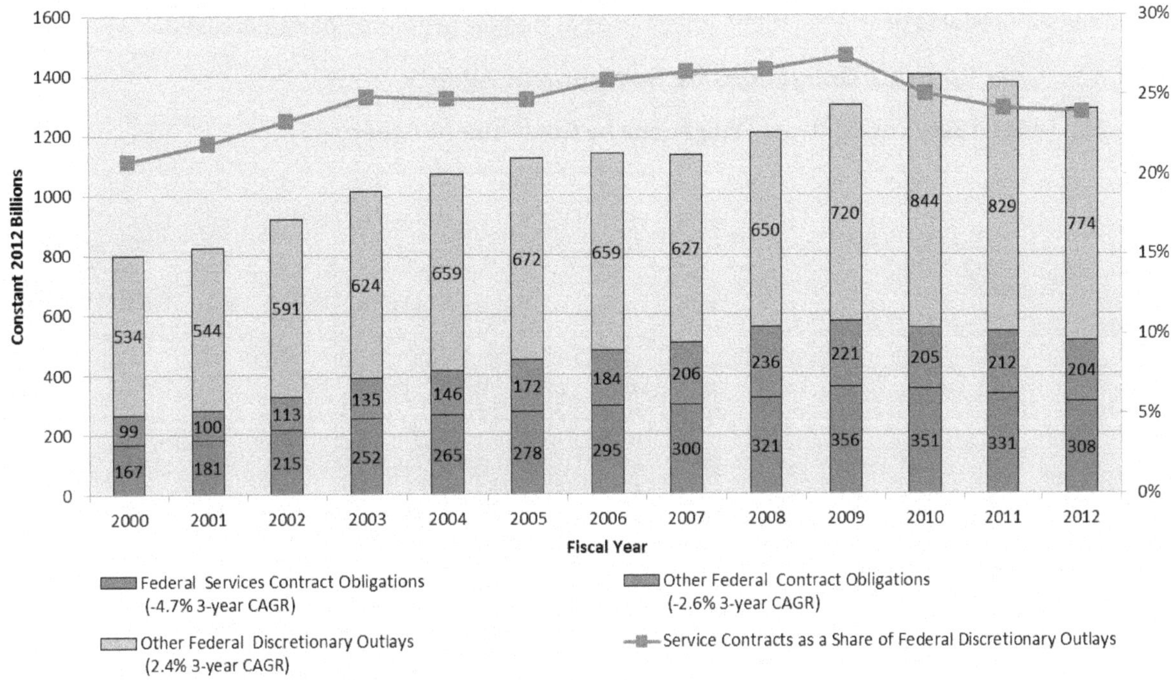

Source: FPDS; OMB Historical Tables; CSIS analysis.

Figure 2-1 presents total federal government obligations from 2000 to 2012, broken down by federal services contract obligations, other federal contract obligations (for products), and other federal discretionary outlays. Contract obligations, as throughout the report, are tracked in FY 2012 dollar amounts. These amounts appear by the data labels on the bars, corresponding with the left-hand y-axis. Federal services contract obligations are tracked as a share of overall federal discretionary outlays by the line near the top of the graph, corresponding with the right-hand y-axis.

Between 2000 and 2012, growth in federal services contract obligations (22.6 percent 12-year compound annual growth rate, or CAGR) and other federal contract obligations (27.5 percent 12-year CAGR) have significantly outpaced overall federal discretionary outlays (17.1 percent 12-year CAGR), while other federal discretionary outlays (13.1 percent 12-year CAGR) have grown more slowly. As a share of overall federal discretionary outlays, federal services contract obligations rose from 21 percent in 2000 to 27 percent in 2009, but have declined since. As a share of total federal contract obligations, federal services contract obligations rose from 63 percent in 2000 to 65 percent in 2004, then declined steadily to 58 percent in 2008 before rebounding to 62 percent in 2009, and have fluctuated since.

In the 2009–2012 period, as overall federal discretionary outlays peaked and then fell (-0.3 percent 3-year CAGR), both federal services contract obligations (-4.7 percent 3-year CAGR) and other federal contract obligations (-2.6 percent 3-year CAGR) saw mild declines. As a share of overall federal contract obligations, federal services contract obligations declined from 62 percent in 2009 to 60 percent in 2012, well within bounds of previous fluctuations. As a share of overall federal discretionary outlays, federal services contract obligations declined from their peak value of 27 percent in 2009 to 24 percent in 2012. Other federal discretionary outlays grew slightly during this period (2.4 percent 3-year CAGR), with stimulus spending leading to a jump in 2010 and 2011.

Between 2011 and 2012, as overall federal discretionary outlays declined by 6 percent, both federal services contract obligations (-7 percent) and other federal discretionary outlays (-7 percent) declined at slightly faster rates. Other federal contract obligations, by contrast, declined at half the overall rate of decline (-3 percent), indicating that federal agencies have prioritized preserving obligations for products over obligations for services as budget pressures have increased.

Federal Services Contract Obligations by Government Agency

Figure 2-2: Federal Services Contract Obligations by Government Agency

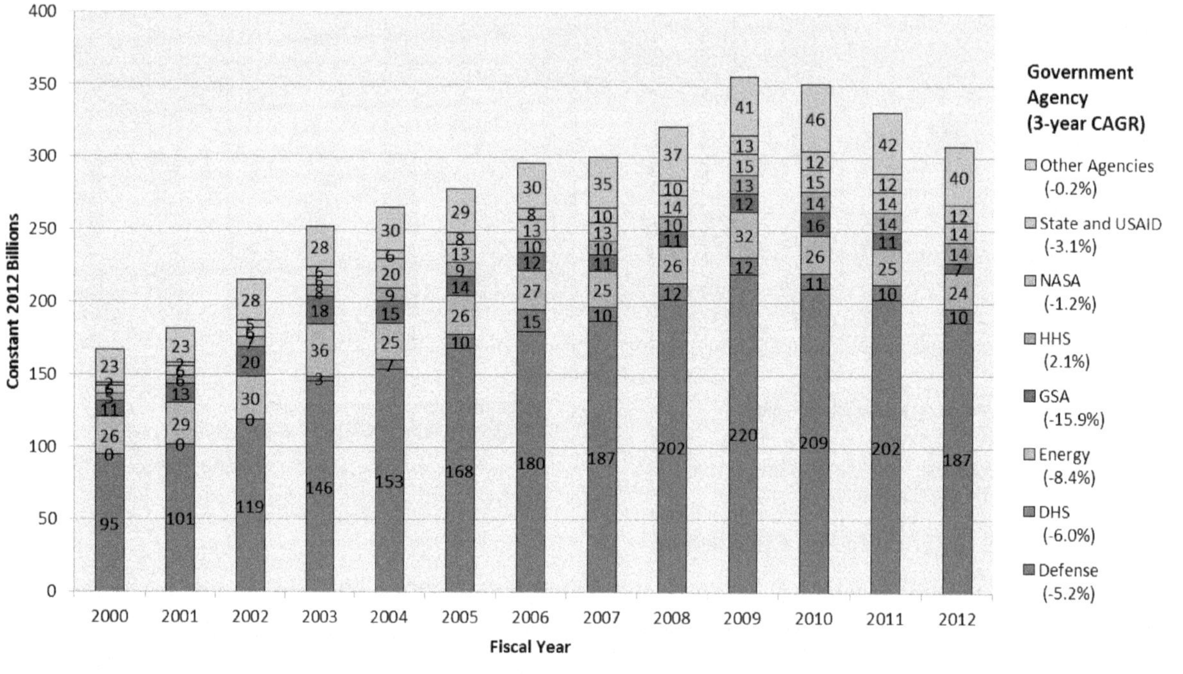

Source: FPDS; CSIS analysis.

From 2000 to 2012, the Department of Defense has controlled a growing majority of federal services contract obligations, rising from $94.6 billion in 2000 (57 percent share) to $219.5 billion in 2009 (62 percent share), before declining in recent years. DHS, created in 2003, rose to account for 5 percent of total federal services contract obligations in 2006 due to the response to Hurricane Katrina, but has not exceeded 4 percent since. DoE, which accounted for between 14 percent and 16 percent of total contract obligations from 2000 to 2003, has declined to between 7 percent and 9 percent since. GSA rose to account for 10 percent of contract obligations in 2002, but has not exceeded 5 percent of contract obligations since 2004.

In the 2009–2012 period, services contract obligations for DoD declined at a -5.2 percent 3-year CAGR, from $219.5 billion to $186.8. Three other agencies saw reductions in their respective services contract obligations larger than those of overall services contract obligations: GSA (-15.9 percent 3-year CAGR), DoE (-8.4 percent 3-year CAGR), and DHS (-6.0 percent 3-year CAGR). State/USAID, NASA, and Other Agencies all saw declines in contract obligations lower than that for overall services contract obligations, and HHS actually saw slight growth (2.1 percent 3-year CAGR).

GSA and DoD experienced notable declines between 2011 and 2012 that merit further discussion. GSA services contract obligations declined from $11.5 billion in 2011 to $7.3 billion in 2012, a 37 percent decrease, almost entirely in FRS&C.[5] The primary driver of this decline is a near disappearance of obligations for "Lease of Office Buildings" (Product or Service Code (PSC) X111/X1AA), which dropped from $4.7 billion in 2010 to $3.2 billion in 2011 to $13 million in 2012. This is apparently the result of a decision by GSA to stop reporting leases of office buildings into FPDS. Though this decision is allowed under FAR 4.606(b)(3), **this represents a large step backwards for data transparency. The research team estimates that these obligations no longer reported to FPDS could make up 39 percent of GSA's services contract obligations, not to mention 1.5 percent of total federal services contract obligations.** See the GSA section of Chapter 4 for more detailed analysis of this issue.

DoD saw a reduction in services contract obligations from $202.4 billion in 2011 to $186.8 billion in 2012, an 8 percent decrease. DoD saw significant declines in contract obligations for FRS&C, PAMS, and R&D. See the DoD section of Chapter 4 for a more detailed breakdown of the specific services that saw notable declines.

Federal Services Contract Obligations by Service Area

Figure 2-3: Federal Services Contract Obligations by Service Area

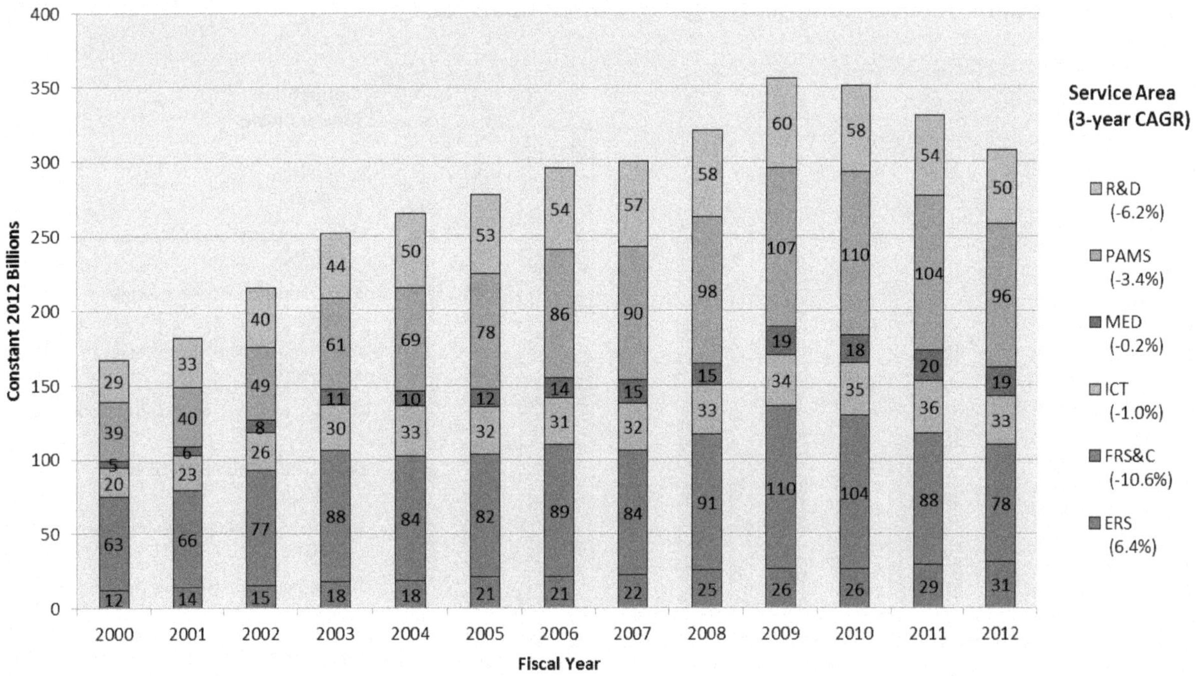

Source: FPDS; CSIS analysis.

From 2000 to 2012, the major shifts in services contract obligations have been in FRS&C and PAMS. FRS&C, which accounted for 37 percent of services contract obligations in 2000, accounted for only 25 percent in 2012. Meanwhile, PAMS, which accounted for 23 percent of services contract obligations in 2000, rose to account for 31 percent in 2012. MED has seen slow but steady growth over the period

[5] GSA contract obligations in 2009 and 2010 were notably inflated by funds from the American Recovery and Reinvestment Act of 2009, which boosted GSA contract obligations for construction and maintenance/repair/alteration of office buildings by $1.2 billion in 2009 and $3.1 billion in 2010.

observed, doubling from 3 percent of services contract obligations in 2000 to 6 percent in 2012. ERS, ICT, and R&D have been relatively stable as shares of overall federal services contracting obligations.

From 2009 to 2012, FRS&C contract obligations declined the most dramatically (-10.6 percent 3-year CAGR), dropping from $109.6 billion in 2009 to $78.4 billion in 2012. R&D also declined more rapidly than overall services contract obligations (-6.2 percent 3-year CAGR), dropping from $60.1 billion in 2009 to $49.5 billion in 2012. PAMS (-3.4 percent 3-year CAGR), ICT (-1.0 percent 3-year CAGR), and MED (-0.2 percent 3-year CAGR) all saw moderate declines in contract obligations, slower than that of overall services contract obligations. ERS contract obligations, by contrast, saw moderate growth since 2009 (6.4 percent 3-year CAGR), rising from $26 billion in 2009 to $31.3 billion in 2012.

ERS was the only service area to see an increase in contract obligations between 2011 and 2012, rising from $29.3 billion to $31.3 billion. ICT and MED saw moderate reductions in contract obligations (7 and 8 percent declines, respectively), while R&D (8 percent) and PAMS (8 percent) saw similar declines and FRS&C (11 percent) saw more severe reductions. As discussed with Figure 2-2, the FRS&C decline is driven by reductions in DoD and GSA, while the PAMS and R&D declines are driven from within DoD.

Federal Services Contract Obligations by Competition

Figure 2-4: Federal Services Contract Obligations by Competition

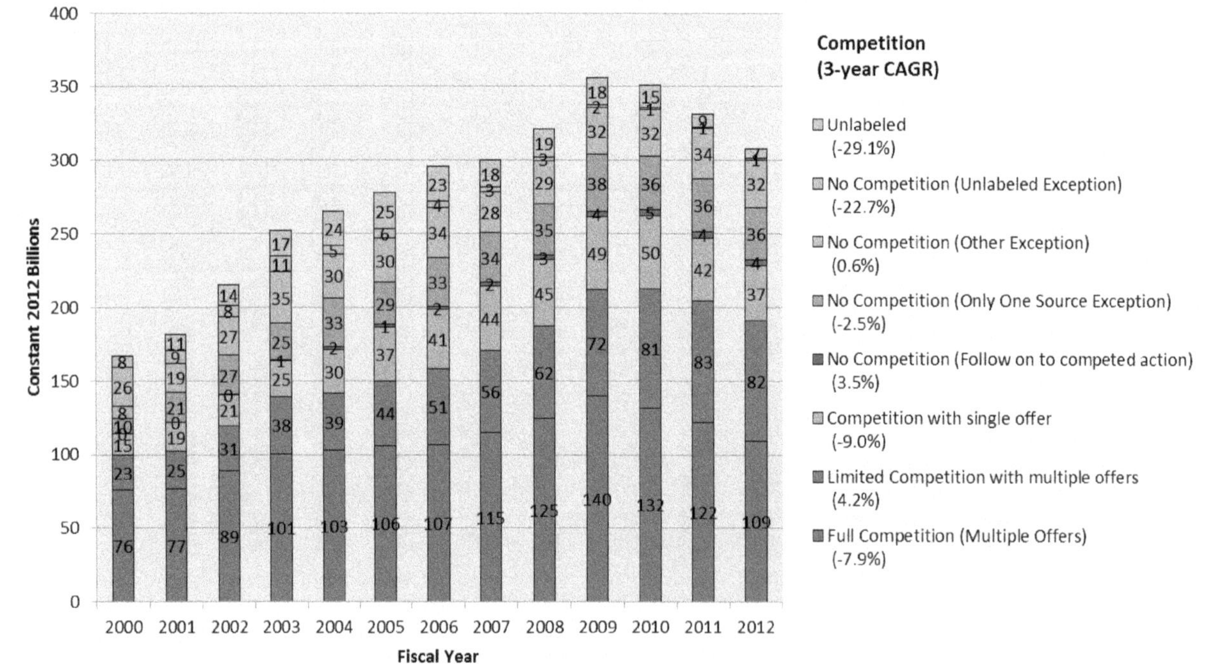

Source: FPDS; CSIS analysis.

From 2000 to 2012, over half of federal services contract obligations have been awarded after competition with multiple offers. The share awarded after competition with multiple offers declined from 60 percent in 2000 to 53 percent in 2004, but has increased steadily since. Within this category, limited competition with multiple offers has grown at over four times the rate of full competition with multiple offers, almost quadrupling in value since 2000. This coincides with an increased use of multiple-award IDCs in services contracting, which are by definition "limited," because each IDC has a pool of vendors that went through a pre-qualification process. This is deceiving, however, as multiple-award

IDCs are usually highly competitive in terms of numbers of offers received on each contract action, as will be explored further in Chapter 5. The share of services contract obligations awarded without competition held steady between 26 percent and 28 percent from 2000 to 2004, then declined steadily through 2010 (to 21 percent) before rebounding in the last two years. The major trend within uncompeted contract obligations has been the decline in contract obligations awarded without competition with no specific exception cited, which declined from nearly 60 percent of all contract obligations labeled "no competition" in 2000 to just over 1 percent in 2012. The share of services contract obligations awarded after competition with a single offer rose steadily through the mid-2000s, from 9 percent in 2000 to 15 percent in 2007, but has declined since, a sign that agencies are doing a better job of soliciting bidders for competitive contract actions. Unlabeled contracts, which accounted for as much as 9 percent of services contract obligations in the mid-2000s, have steadily declined since.

From 2009 to 2012, contract obligations awarded after competition with multiple offers declined at a -3.4 percent 3-year CAGR, similar to the rate of decline for overall services contract obligations. Within the category, full and open competition declined more rapidly (-7.9 percent 3-year CAGR), while limited competition with multiple offers showed mild growth (4.2 percent 3-year CAGR). During the same period, the share of contract obligations awarded after competition with multiple offers increased from 60 percent in 2009 to 62 percent in 2012. Contract obligations awarded without competition decreased at a -1.4 percent 3-year CAGR, less than a third of the rate of decline for services contract obligations overall. The share of services contract obligations awarded without competition increased from 21 percent in 2009 to 24 percent in 2012. Contract obligations awarded after competition with a single offer declined at a -9.0 percent 3-year CAGR, dropping as a share of overall services contract obligations from 14 percent in 2009 to 12 percent in 2012. Unlabeled contracts continued their decline, at a -29.1 percent 3-year CAGR.

Between 2011 and 2012, the share of services contract obligations awarded after competition with multiple offers held steady at 62 percent, while competition with a single offer declined from 13 percent to 12 percent, and no competition increased from 23 percent to 24 percent.

Federal Services Contract Obligations by Funding Mechanism

Figure 2-5: Federal Services Contract Obligations by Funding Mechanism

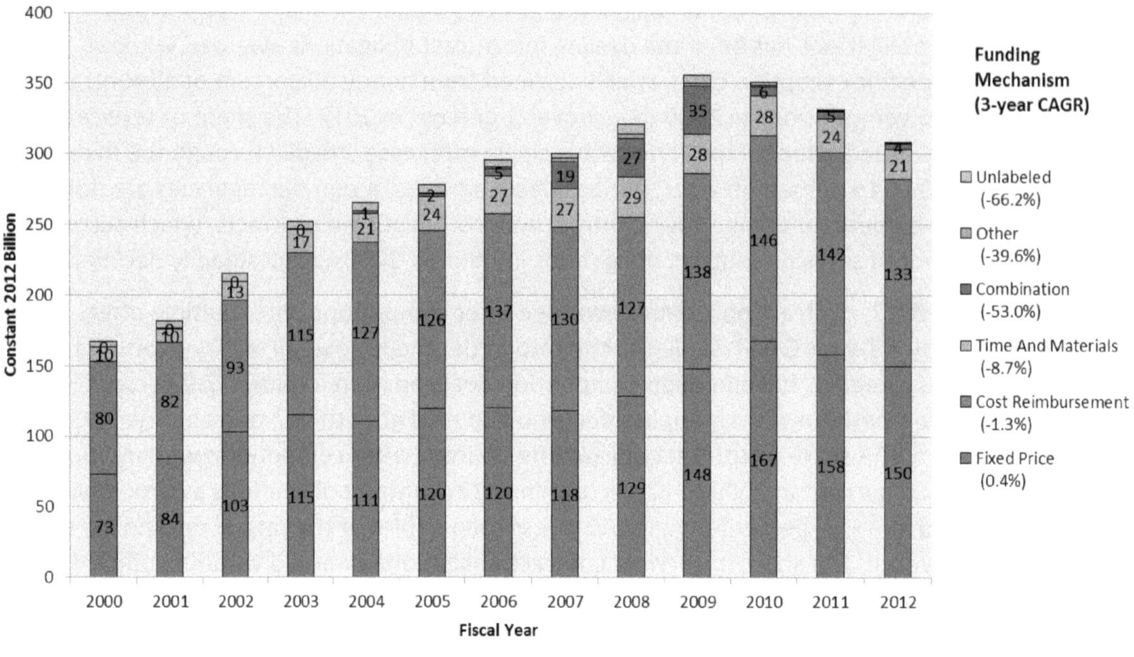

Source: FPDS; CSIS analysis.

The use of fixed price contract types declined steadily from 2002 to 2007 as a share of federal services contract obligations, dropping from 48 percent in 2002 to 39 percent in 2007. The share of services, contract obligations awarded under fixed price contract types has increased since, to 49 percent in 2012, in line with OMB guidance to increase the use of fixed price contract types across the federal government. The share of services contract obligations awarded under cost reimbursement contract types, which declined steadily for most of the decade (from 48 percent in 2000 to 39 percent in 2009), has risen since, to 43 percent in 2012. The share of services contract obligations awarded under time and materials contracts has accounted for between 7 percent and 9 percent of total services contract obligations in every year since 2003.

From 2009 to 2012, contract obligations awarded under fixed price contract types showed very minor growth (0.4 percent 3-year CAGR), in large part due to better data labeling, while contract obligations awarded under cost reimbursement contract types declined slightly (-1.3 percent 3-year CAGR). Contract obligations awarded under time and materials contracts, by contrast, declined moderately (-8.7 percent 3-year CAGR), at nearly twice the rate of overall services contract obligations. Between 2011 and 2012, the share of contract obligations awarded under fixed price contract types increased slightly (from 48 percent in 2011 to 49 percent in 2012), while cost reimbursement and time and materials contract types held steady at 43 percent and 7 percent, respectively.

It is worth noting the significant progress made across the federal government in data quality in the period observed. Contract obligations classified as "other," which accounted for $3.1 billion in 2008, accounted for only $300 million in 2012. Unlabeled contract obligations, which accounted for $6.3 billion in 2008, accounted for only $200 million in 2012. Particularly encouraging is the rapid decline in the use of the combination contracts category, in line with federal guidance. As discussed in previous contracting analysis from CSIS, combination contracts are those with elements of more than one funding mechanism type, and the use of the category hindered analysis. After accounting for 10 percent of all services contract obligations in 2009, they dropped to 2 percent in 2010, and only 1 percent in 2012.

Federal Services Contract Obligations by Contract Vehicle

Figure 2-6: Federal Services Contract Obligations by Contract Vehicle

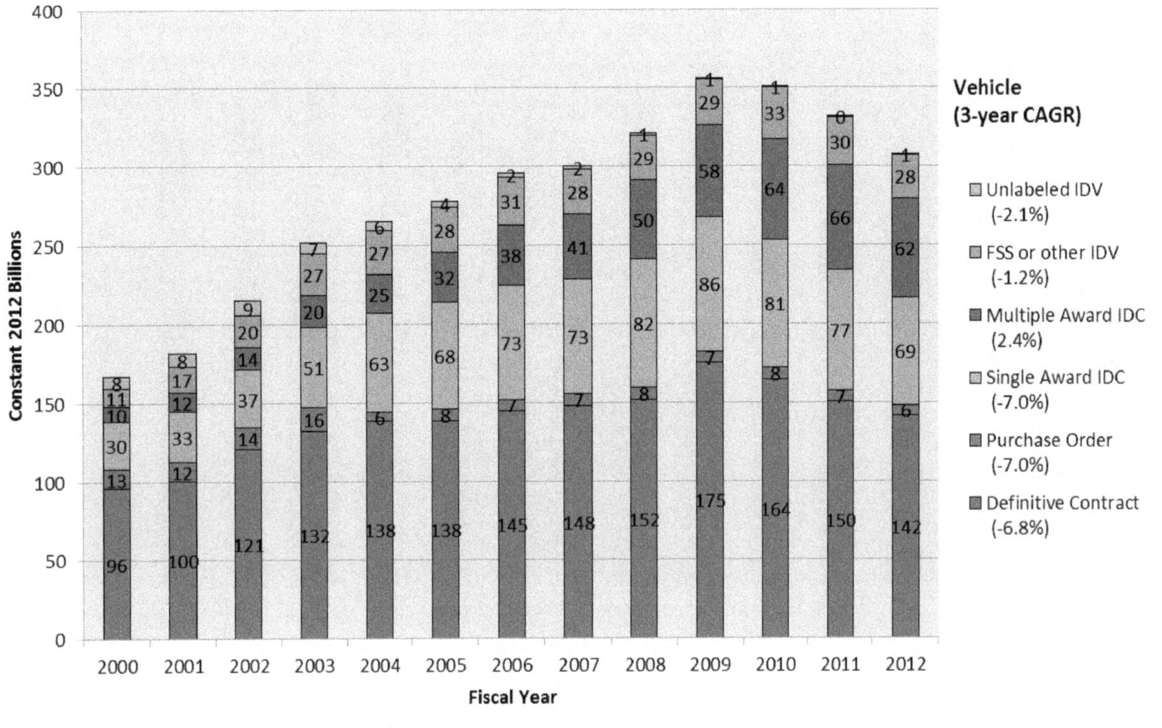

Source: FPDS; CSIS analysis.

Between 2000 and 2012, the use of definitive contracts in federal services contracting has steadily decreased. From accounting for 57 percent of services contracting obligations in 2000, the share of services contract obligations awarded under definitive contracts fell to 46 percent in 2012. Purchase orders, which accounted for 8 percent of services contract obligations in 2000, have not exceeded 3 percent since 2003. The share of services contract obligations awarded under multiple-award IDCs has more than tripled, from 6 percent in 2000 to 20 percent in 2012. Single-award IDCs rose from 18 percent of services contract obligations in 2000 to 26 percent in 2008, but have declined steadily since, to 22 percent in 2012. FSS and other IDVs have accounted for between 9 percent and 11 percent of services contract obligations for most of the period, while unlabeled IDVs have steadily declined, accounting for less than 1 percent of services contract obligations in every year since 2006.

From 2009 to 2012, contract obligations for three types of vehicles declined more rapidly than did overall services contract obligations: single-award IDCs (-7.0 percent 3-year CAGR), purchase orders (-7.0 percent 3-year CAGR), and definitive contracts (-6.8 percent 3-year CAGR). Contract obligations awarded under FSS or other IDVs declined more slowly than did overall services contract obligations (-1.2 percent 3-year CAGR), and multiple-award IDCs actually increased slightly in the 2009–2012 period (2.4 percent 3-year CAGR).

Between 2011 and 2012, the use of contract vehicles in federal services contract obligations saw only minor changes. The share of contract obligations awarded under definitive contracts rose from 45 percent in 2011 to 46 percent in 2012, while single-award IDCs declined from 23 percent in 2011 to 22 percent in 2012. Multiple-award IDCs, purchase orders, and FSS and other IDVs held steady at 20 percent, 2 percent, and 9 percent, respectively.

Federal Services Contract Obligations by Vendor Size

Figure 2-7: Federal Services Contract Obligations by Vendor Size

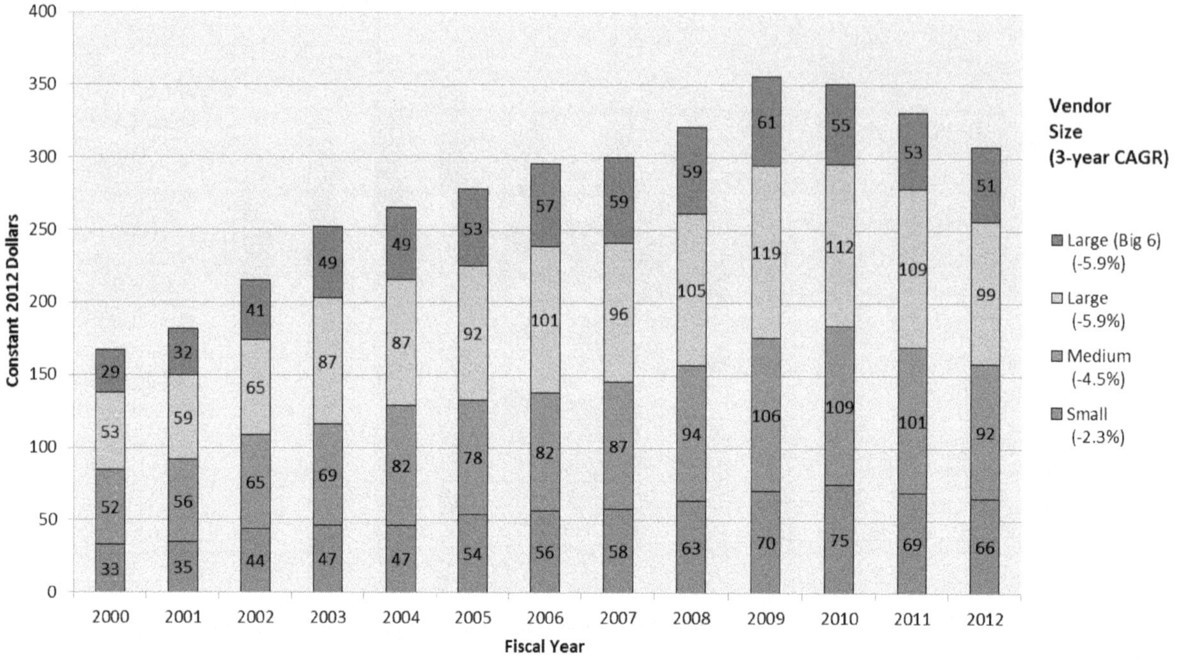

Source: FPDS; CSIS analysis.

Between 2000 and 2012, the shares of federal services contract obligations going to small, medium, large, and the Big 6 vendors have been remarkably consistent. Small vendors have accounted for between 18 percent and 21 percent of contract obligations throughout the period observed, though that share has been growing slowly since the mid-2000s. Medium vendors have accounted for between 28 and 31 percent of contract obligations throughout the period observed, again with the trend of small increases since the mid-2000s. Large vendors have accounted for between 32 percent and 34 percent of contract obligations in every year except 2002 (30 percent), with a slight decline since the mid-2000s. The Big 6 vendors accounted for between 17 percent and 20 percent of contract obligations from 2000 to 2009, but have declined somewhat since.

From 2009 to 2012, contract obligations awarded to small vendors declined at less than half the rate of overall services contract obligations (-2.3 percent 3-year CAGR). Both large vendors and the Big 6 declined at the same rate (-5.9 percent 3-year CAGR), slightly faster than the rate of decline for overall services contract obligations. Contract obligations awarded to medium vendors declined at a rate similar to that of overall services contract obligations (-4.5 percent 3-year CAGR). This seems to contradict the conventional wisdom of a so-called mid-tier squeeze, as since 2009, the services contracting market for medium-sized vendors has declined more slowly than for large and Big 6 vendors.

Between 2011 and 2012, as overall services contract obligations declined by 7 percent, medium vendors (-8 percent) and large vendors (-9 percent) declined slightly faster, while small vendors (-5 percent) declined somewhat more slowly. The Big 6 (-3 percent), meanwhile, declined at a rate notably slower than that of overall services contract obligations, indicating that the biggest vendors seem to be having the most success at preserving their market shares of federal services contract obligations during the current budget drawdown. By shares of services contract obligations, small vendors (21 percent) and medium vendors (30 percent) held steady, while large vendors declined slightly (33 percent in 2011, 32 percent in 2012) and the Big 6 saw slight growth (16 percent in 2011, 17 percent in 2012.)

Federal Services Contract Obligations by Contract Size

Figure 2-8: Federal Services Contract Obligations by Contract Size

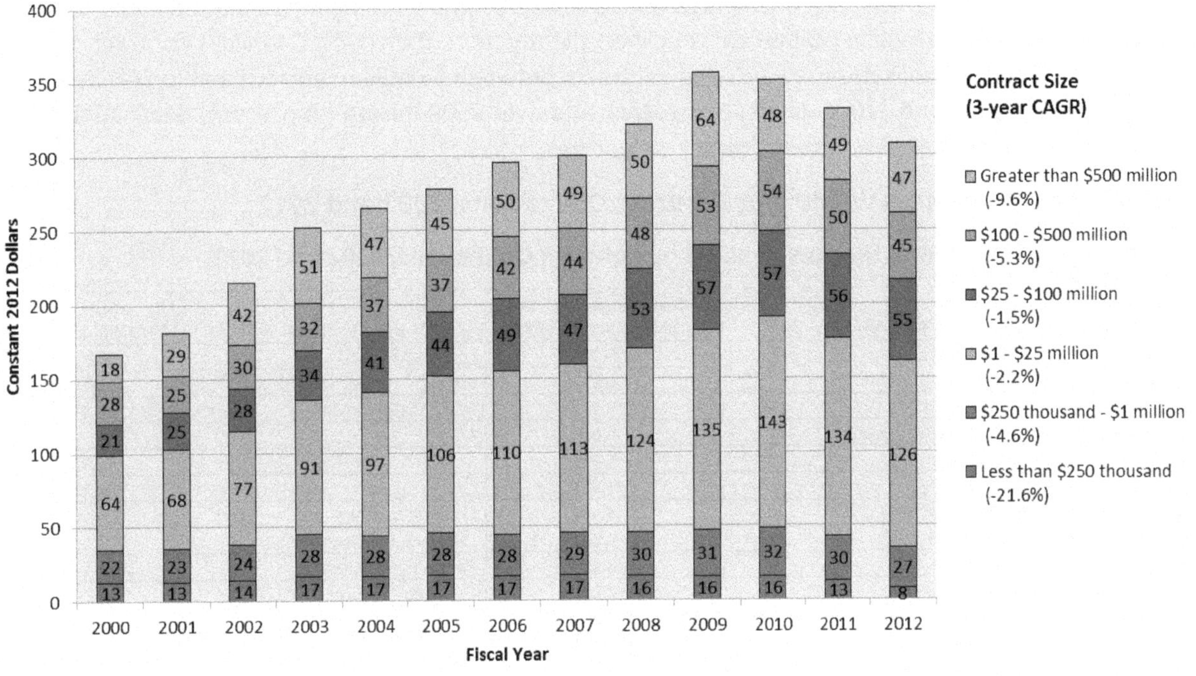

Source: FPDS; CSIS analysis.

For this and all other discussions of contract size in this report, "contract size" classifications are based on the total contract obligations under a given contract for the fiscal year in question, not the total value of the contract.

From 2000 to 2012, there has been a trend of decreasing services contract obligations awarded as part of contracts under $1 million and over $500 million, and increasing contract obligations for contracts between $1 million and $25 million and between $25 million and $100 million. Contracts for less than $250,000, which accounted for 8 percent of services contract obligations in 2000, declined to only 3 percent by 2012. Similarly, the share of contract obligations awarded in contracts between $250,000 and $1 million declined from 13 percent in 2000 to 9 percent in 2012. Contracts for greater than $500 million rose from 11 percent of contract obligations in 2000 to 20 percent in 2003, but have declined since, to 15 percent in 2012. Contracts for between $1 million and $25 million, which accounted for 36 percent of contract obligations from 2002 to 2004, grew to account for 41 percent of contract obligations by 2012. The share of services contract obligations awarded in contracts between $25 million and $100 million grew steadily through the decade, from 13 percent in 2000 to 18 percent in 2012. Services contract obligations awarded in contracts between $100 million and $500 million held steady between 13 percent and 15 percent in every year since 2000.

From 2009 to 2012, services contract obligations for contracts under $250,000 declined at a -21.6 3-year CAGR. Contract obligations for contracts greater than $500 million also declined sharply

(-9.6 percent 3-year CAGR). Two other categories declined at rates similar to the rate of decline for services contract obligations overall: $250,000 to $1 million (-4.6 percent 3-year CAGR) and $100 million to $500 million (-5.3 percent 3-year CAGR). Services contract obligations awarded in contracts between $1 million and $25 million (-2.2 percent 3-year CAGR) and between $25 million and $100 million (-1.5 percent 3-year CAGR) declined at a rate slower than that of overall services contract obligations.

Between 2011 and 2012, services contract obligations awarded in contracts under $250,000 dropped by 39 percent, over five times the rate of decline for services contract obligations overall. Contract obligations awarded in contracts between $250,000 and $1 million (-10 percent) and between $100 million and $500 million (-9 percent) declined slightly more than overall services contract obligations. Contract obligations awarded in contracts between $1 million and $25 million (-6 percent), between $25 million and $100 million (-3 percent), and over $500 million (-3 percent) declined at a rate slower than that of overall services contract obligations.

Top 20 Federal Services Vendors by Contract Obligations, 2002 and 2012

Table 2-1: Top 20 Federal Services Vendors by Contract Obligations, 2002 and 2012

Rank	Top 20 Vendors in 2002	Obligations in 2002 Millions	2001 Rank	Top 20 Vendors in 2012	Obligations in 2012 Millions	2011 Rank
1	Lockheed Martin	15,000	1	Lockheed Martin	17,970	1
2	University Of California	9,510	2	Boeing	9,850	3
3	Boeing	8,050	3	Northrop Grumman	9,260	2
4	Northrop Grumman	6,020	9	SAIC	6,760	4
5	Raytheon	5,320	6	Raytheon	6,430	5
Subtotal for Top 5		**43,910**			**50,280**	
6	General Dynamics	4,630	5	General Dynamics	4,500	6
7	Bechtel	4,230	7	L3 Communications	4,350	8
8	SAIC	3,900	4	Booz Allen Hamilton	4,040	9
9	ASDV	2,980	-	Computer Sciences Corp.	3,900	7
10	Dyncorp International	2,640	17	Dyncorp International	3,540	10
11	TRW	2,610	8	Humana	3,470	12
12	Computer Sciences Corp.	2,500	11	URS	3,470	14
13	Health Net	2,120	19	Bechtel	3,300	11
14	BAE Systems	1,960	15	Health Net	3,140	16
15	Acepex Management	1,850	-	BAE Systems	3,110	15
16	United Technologies	1,780	21	TriWest Healthcare	3,010	17
17	Washington Savannah River Company*	1,780	12	Battelle	2,290	23
18	Humana	1,630	46	CACI	2,270	20
19	Booz Allen Hamilton	1,400	23	Hewlett-Packard	2,220	19
20	Electronic Data Systems	1,340	31	ITT	2,200	13
Total for Top 20		**81,250**			**99,100**	
Total for all industry		**214,880**			**307,750**	

* Joint Venture; - Outside the top 100 vendors

Source: FPDS; CSIS analysis.

Five of the Big 6 vendors were among the top 6 recipients of federal services contract obligations in both 2002 and 2012, in roughly the same order: Lockheed Martin, Boeing, Northrop Grumman, Raytheon, and General Dynamics. The University of California, which accounted for the second-most contract obligations in 2002 (based on large contracts for managing government nuclear research facilities), was replaced in the top 5 by SAIC, which grew from 8th in 2002 to 4th in 2012. Overall, the top 5 services vendors accounted for 20 percent of services contract obligations in 2002, but only 16 percent in 2012.

The rest of the top 20 shows an increase in the number of IT and medical firms since 2002, reflecting the increased obligations in those areas across the federal government. Overall, the share of total federal services contract obligations awarded to the top 10 vendors declined from 29 percent in

2002 to 23 percent in 2012, and the share awarded to the top 20 declined from 38 percent in 2002 to 32 percent in 2012. Similarly, within the top 20, the share of contract obligations awarded to the top 5 vendors has declined, from 54 percent in 2002 to 51 percent in 2012. Overall, the decreasing shares of federal services contract obligations awarded to top vendors suggest an increasingly open market for medium-sized firms and firms that are not traditionally government vendors to participate meaningfully in the federal services marketplace.

There was remarkably little change in the composition or ordering of the top 20 between 2011 and 2012, with only one vendor outside the top 20 in 2011 making it into the top 20 in 2012 (Battelle, which was ranked 23rd in 2011). The vendor that saw the biggest drop within the top 20 was ITT, which fell from 13th in 2011 to 20th in 2012.

Chapter 3: Contracting for Federal Services by Service Area

This chapter presents data for each of the six service areas analyzed in this study: Information and Communication Technology services; Professional, Administrative, and Management Support services; Research and Development services; Equipment-Related Services; Facilities-Related Services & Construction; and Medical services. For each, the analysis includes data on federal government agencies, the level of competition, and types of funding mechanism and contract vehicle used. It also includes an analysis of the industrial base for each service area, including: top 10 vendor lists for each service area for 2012 (with 2011 ranks for each vendor); analysis of cross-area participation among all federal services vendors in 2002 and 2012; and analysis of cross-area participation among the overall top 20 federal services vendors in 2002 and 2012.

Figure 3-1: The Federal Information and Communications Technology Services Market, 2000–2012

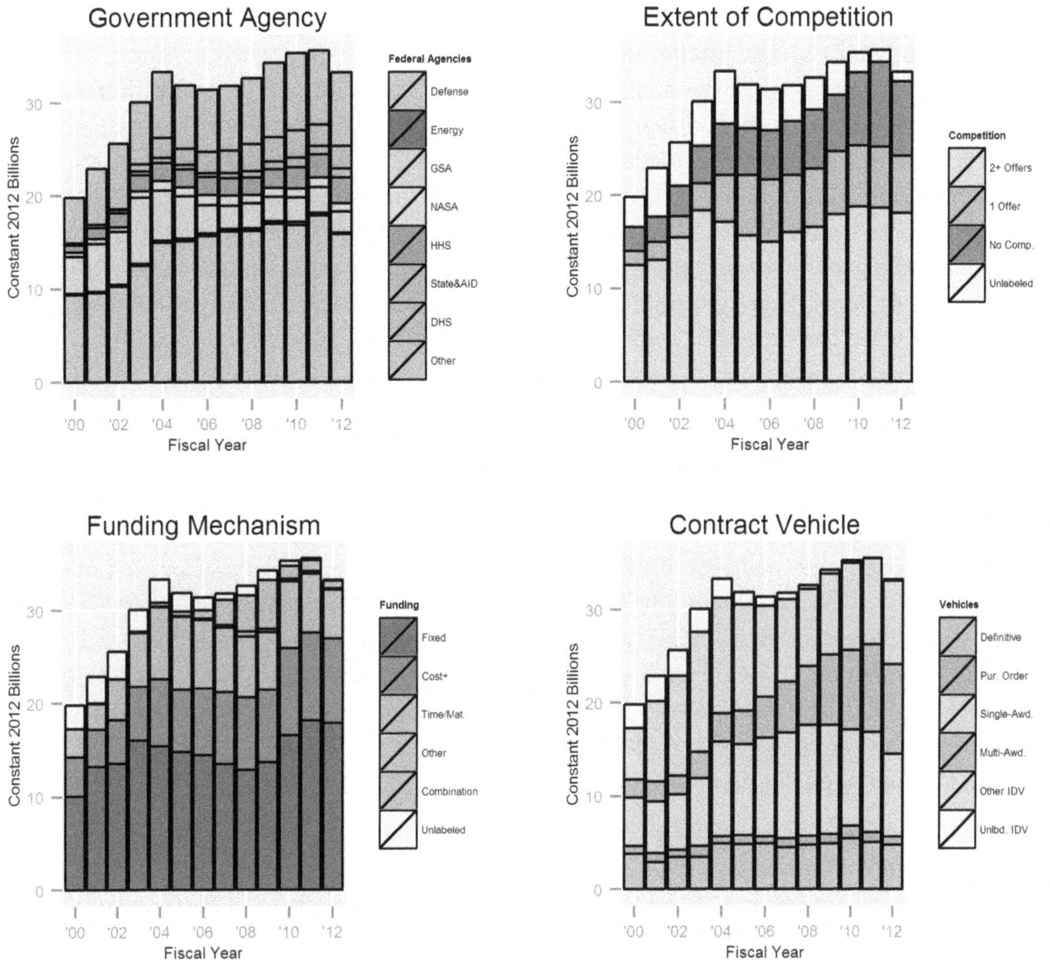

Top 10 Vendors

Vendor	2012 Millions	2011 Rank
SAIC	2,320	2
Lockheed Martin	1,960	3
Hewlett-Packard	1,940	1
Northrop Grumman	1,430	5
Computer Sciences Corp.	1,370	4
General Dynamics	1,260	7
IBM	800	6
Harris	760	11
Booz Allen Hamilton	690	10
Accenture	600	12
Top 10 ICT Obligations	16,920	
Total ICT Obligations	33,270	

* Joint Venture

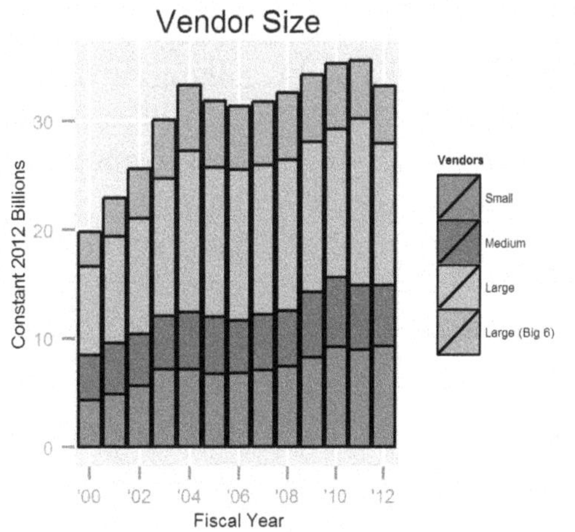

Source: FPDS; CSIS analysis.

ICT

From 2000 to 2012, DoD has accounted for between two-fifths and half of ICT contract obligations, while no other single agency accounted for more than 10 percent after 2006 (GSA had accounted for over 20 percent in the early 2000s). Over half of ICT contract obligations were awarded after competition with multiple offers in all but one year in the period observed, though competition with a single offer has risen steadily to account for over a quarter of ICT contract obligations. The majority of ICT contract obligations have been awarded under fixed price contract types throughout the period observed, though cost reimbursement and time and materials contracts are also prevalent. FSS and other IDVs were the most common contract vehicles for ICT in the early 2000s, but moderate growth in single-award IDCs and rapid growth in multiple-award IDCs led to roughly equal shares for the three vehicle categories in recent years. Large vendors have accounted for the largest share of ICT contract obligations throughout the period observed, with slow but steady growth in contract obligations awarded to small vendors.

From 2009 to 2012, ICT contract obligations declined at a -1 percent 3-year CAGR. Between 2011 and 2012, ICT contract obligations declined by 6 percent.

Government Agency

In the 2009–2012 period, DoE saw the most dramatic decline in ICT contract obligations (-21.4 percent 3-year CAGR), albeit from a high of just over $300 million. GSA showed a moderate decline in ICT contract obligations (-5.2 percent 3-year CAGR), while DHS (-2.8 percent 3-year CAGR), DoD (-2.1 percent 3-year CAGR), and NASA (-1.4 percent 3-year CAGR) experienced slight declines at rates faster than the decline in overall ICT contract obligations. State/USAID saw mild growth (4.3 percent 3-year CAGR), while HHS saw strong growth over the 2009–2012 period (11.9 percent 3-year CAGR). ICT contract obligations in other agencies were stagnant.

Between 2011 and 2012, as overall ICT contract obligations declined 6 percent, four agencies declined more sharply: DoE (-43 percent), GSA (-20 percent), DoD (-11 percent), and NASA (-7 percent). Three other agencies showed growth in ICT contract obligations: DHS (5 percent), HHS (9 percent), and State/USAID (11 percent).

Competition

In the 2009–2012 period, ICT contract obligations awarded after competition with multiple offers were stagnant (0.3 percent 3-year CAGR). Contract obligations awarded without competition, by contrast, grew steadily (9.6 percent 3-year CAGR), rising as a share of ICT contract obligations from 18 percent in 2009 to 24 percent in 2012. This rise in uncompeted contract obligations appears to be the result of better data labeling, as it coincides with a sharp decline in unlabeled contract obligations (-32.1 percent 3-year CAGR), which declined from 10 percent in 2009 to 3 percent in 2012. ICT contract obligations awarded after competition with a single offer declined slightly over the period in question (-3.3 percent 3-year CAGR), declining as a share of overall ICT contract obligations from 20 percent in 2009 to 18 percent in 2012.

Between 2011 and 2012, this trend seemed to reverse: the share of ICT contract obligations awarded after competition with multiple offers rose from 52 percent to 54 percent, while the share awarded without competition declined from 26 percent to 24 percent. The share awarded after competition with a single offer held steady.

Funding Mechanism

In the 2009–2012 period, ICT contract obligations awarded under fixed price contract types increased at a 9.4 percent 3-year CAGR, rising from 40 percent of ICT contract obligations in 2009 to 54 percent in 2012. Contract obligations awarded under cost reimbursement contract types grew more slowly (5.2 percent 3-year CAGR), rising from 23 percent of contract obligations in 2009 to 27 percent in 2012. Much of this increase can be attributed to the decline in the use of the combination contract category (-45.2 percent 3-year CAGR), so much of the growth in fixed price and cost reimbursement appears to be due more to improvements in data quality than specific contracting policy changes. ICT contract obligations awarded under time and materials contract types declined at a -5.7 percent 3-year CAGR.

Between 2011 and 2012, the share of ICT contract obligations awarded under fixed price contract types increased from 51 percent to 54 percent, while cost reimbursement held steady and time and materials declined from 18 percent to 16 percent.

Contract Vehicle

In the 2009–2012 period, ICT contract obligations awarded under single-award IDCs declined at a -8.7 percent 3-year CAGR, dropping from 34 percent of contract obligations in 2009 to 27 percent in 2012. Purchase orders also declined faster than overall ICT contract obligations (-5.8 percent 3-year CAGR). ICT contract obligations awarded under definitive contracts declined roughly on pace with overall ICT contract obligations (-0.9 percent 3-year CAGR), while FSS and other IDVs showed slight growth (1.1 percent 3-year CAGR). Multiple-award IDCs showed solid growth over the period observed (8.4 percent 3-year CAGR), rising from 22 percent of ICT contract obligations in 2009 to 29 percent in 2012.

Between 2011 and 2012, the shares of ICT contract obligations awarded under definitive contracts and purchase orders held steady, while multiple-award IDCs (26 percent to 29 percent) and FSS and other IDVs (26 percent to 27 percent) increased, and single-award IDCs (30 percent to 27 percent) decreased.

Vendor Size

In the 2009–2012 period, ICT contract obligations awarded to small vendors grew at a 3.8 percent 3-year CAGR, the only size category that saw growth during this period. Medium vendors (-2.3 percent 3-year CAGR) and large vendors (-1.9 percent 3-year CAGR) both declined at rates comparable to that of overall ICT contract obligations. Contract obligations awarded to the Big 6 vendors declined more steeply than did overall ICT contract obligations (-4.6 percent 3-year CAGR).

Between 2011 and 2012, the share of ICT contract obligations awarded to small vendors increased from 25 percent to 28 percent, while the share awarded to large firms declined from 43 percent to 39 percent. The share of contract obligations awarded to medium vendors increased from 16 percent to 17 percent, while the share awarded to the Big 6 increased from 15 percent to 16 percent. Contract obligations awarded to large firms declined by 15 percent between 2011 and 2012, while contract obligations awarded to small firms increased by 3 percent. Big 6 firms saw only a 1 percent decline in contract obligations, while medium firms saw a 5 percent decline, similar to the decline in overall ICT contract obligations.

Top 10

The top vendors for ICT remained relatively steady between 2002 and 2012, but there was some notable turnover. Electronic Data Systems, ranked fourth in 2002, was acquired by HP, which ranks third in 2012. Harris, which was not in the top 20 in 2002, and Accenture, which was, moved into the top 10 in 2012, while CACI dropped just out of the top 10, and Dyncorp International dropped out of the top 20 entirely.

The share of overall ICT contract obligations awarded to the top 5 vendors held steady at 27 percent between 2002 and 2012, while the share going to the top 10 declined slightly, from 40 percent in 2002 to 39 percent in 2012.

The top 5 ICT vendors stayed consistent between 2011 and 2012, although there was significant reordering. In the rest of the 2012 top 20, there were some notable shifts, with three companies moving up from outside the top 20: CGI (22nd in 2011, 14th in 2012), Dell (21st in 2011, 18th in 2012), and Deloitte (30th in 2011, 19th in 2012). The biggest decline was for ITT, which fell from 9th in 2011 to 16th in 2012, most likely due to ITT spinning off its defense technology business in October 2011, forming Exelis Inc.

Figure 3-2: The Federal Professional, Administrative, and Management Support Services Market, 2000–2012

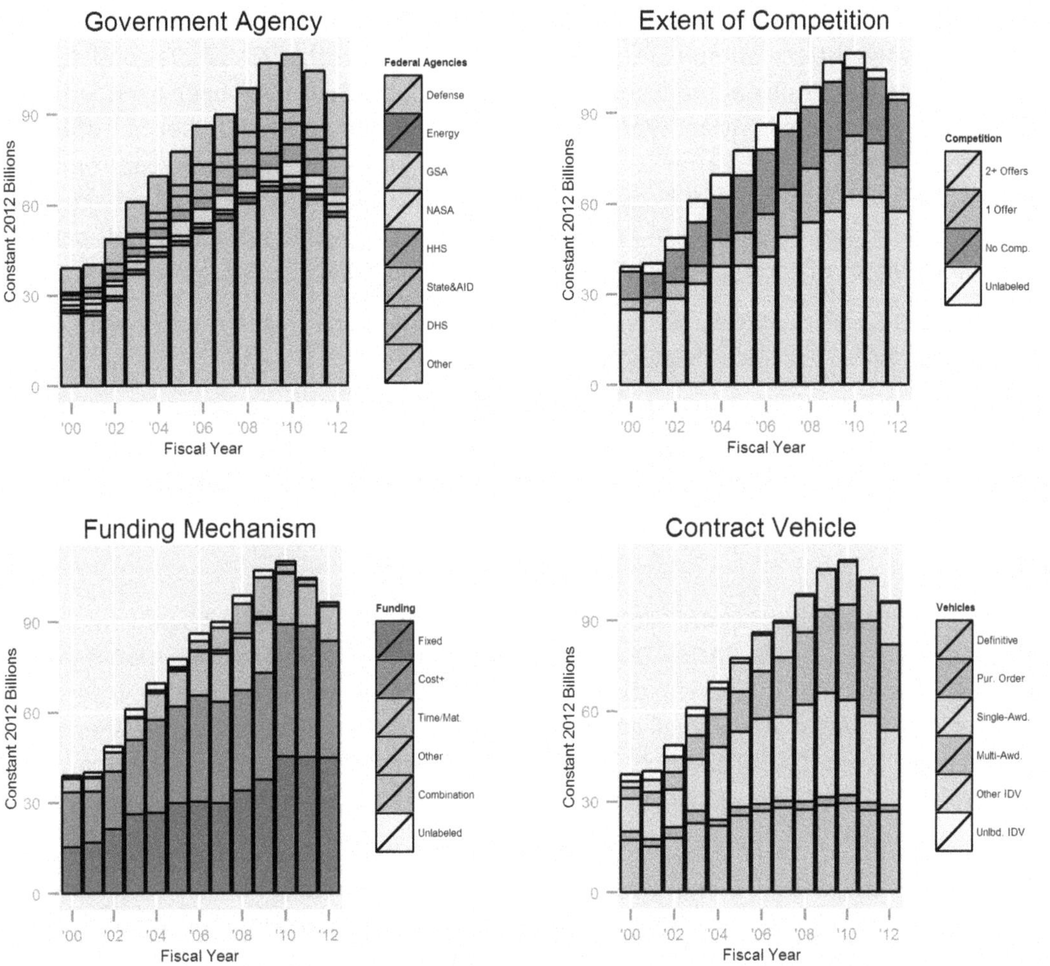

Top 10 Vendors

Vendor	2012 Millions	2011 Rank
Lockheed Martin	3,500	1
Northrop Grumman	2,850	2
Boeing	2,620	12
SAIC	2,440	3
Dyncorp International	2,220	5
Booz Allen Hamilton	2,180	7
Fluor	1,940	4
Computer Sciences Corp.	1,820	6
L3 Communications	1,680	9
CACI	1,500	10
Top 10 PAMS Obligations	33,090	
Total PAMS Obligations	96,250	

* Joint Venture

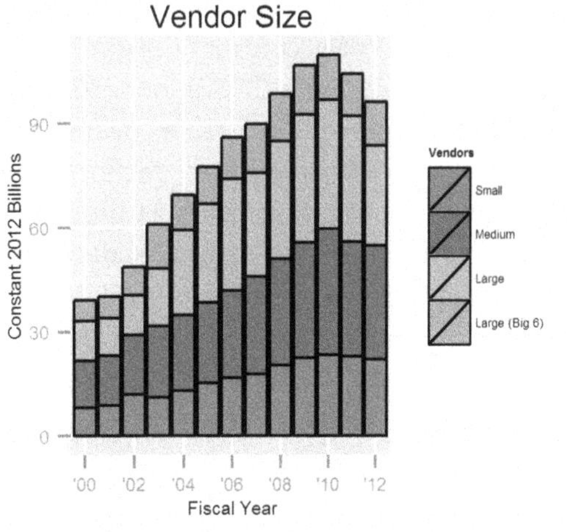

Source: FPDS; CSIS analysis.

PAMS

Between 2000 and 2012, DoD accounted for approximately three-fifths of PAMS contract obligations in every year, while no other single agency accounted for more than 7 percent in any year. Definitive contracts (44 percent) were the most common vehicle for PAMS contract obligations in 2000, but their use has declined since, while the use of multiple-award IDCs and FSS and other IDVs have consistently grown throughout the decade. Similar amounts of PAMS contract obligations have been awarded under fixed price and cost reimbursement contract types throughout the period observed. Over half of PAMS contract obligations have been awarded after competition with multiple offers in every year from 2000 to 2012, and competition with a single offer has grown significantly through the period observed. Large vendors have accounted for over 30 percent of PAMS contract obligations in most years in this period, with roughly consistent shares of contract obligations awarded to the other size categories.

From 2009 to 2012, federal PAMS contract obligations declined at a -3.4 percent 3-year CAGR. Between 2011 and 2012, PAMS contract obligations declined by 8 percent.

Note that PAMS contract obligations were temporarily inflated in 2009 and 2010 due to the American Recovery and Reinvestment Act (ARRA) of 2009, which accounted for 2 percent of PAMS contract obligations in 2009 and 2010. See Chapter 5 for further discussion of the impact of ARRA on services contract trends.

Government Agency

In the 2009–2012 period, PAMS contract obligations declined sharply within DHS (-13.3 percent 3-year CAGR) and NASA (-11.6 percent 3-year CAGR). DoD (-4.6 percent 3-year CAGR) and State/USAID (-4.2 percent 3-year CAGR) saw declines in line with that of overall PAMS contract obligations. DoE declined slightly (-1.5 percent 3-year CAGR), while small increases in PAMS contract obligations were seen in other agencies (1 percent 3-year CAGR) and HHS (3.6 percent 3-year CAGR). GSA, by contrast, saw extremely strong growth in PAMS contract obligations, growing at a 21.2 percent 3-year CAGR.

Between 2011 and 2012, declines larger than that of overall PAMS contract obligations were seen for NASA (-19 percent) and DHS (-14 percent). Defense and other agencies declined at rates similar to overall PAMS contract obligations, while GSA and HHS held steady. PAMS contract obligations for DoE and State/USAID each increased by approximately 3 percent between 2011 and 2012.

Competition

In the 2009–2012 period, PAMS contract obligations awarded after competition with multiple offers were stagnant (0.0 percent 3-year CAGR), nonetheless rising from 54 percent of overall PAMS contract obligations in 2009 to 60 percent in 2012 as overall PAMS contract obligations declined. Contract obligations awarded without competition declined slightly (-0.8 percent 3-year CAGR), rising as a share of overall PAMS contract obligations from 21 percent in 2009 to 23 percent in 2012. Contract obligations awarded after competition with a single offer declined sharply (-9.8 percent 3-year CAGR), a rate of decline almost three times that of overall PAMS contract obligations. As a share of PAMS contract obligations, competition with a single offer declined from 19 percent in 2009 to 15 percent in 2012. Unlabeled, which accounted for 6 percent of contract obligations in 2009, fell to 2 percent in 2012.

Between 2011 and 2012, the share of PAMS contract obligations awarded after competition with multiple offers held steady at 60 percent, while no competition rose from 21 percent to 23 percent, and competition with a single offer dropped from 17 percent to 15 percent.

Funding Mechanism

In the 2009–2012 period, PAMS contract obligations awarded under fixed price contract types increased at a 5.9 percent 3-year CAGR, rising from 35 percent of contract obligations in 2009 to 47 percent in 2012. Cost reimbursement contract types grew more slowly (3.2 percent 3-year CAGR), rising from 33 percent of contract obligations in 2009 to 40 percent in 2012. A major factor in the growth of both categories was the decline of combination contract, which dropped from 12 percent of PAMS contract obligations in 2009 to 2 percent or less in every year since. Both unlabeled and other have also declined sharply in recent years, in line with government-wide data quality initiatives. Time and materials contracts have declined sharply during this period as well (-13.4 percent 3-year CAGR), dropping from 17 percent of PAMS contract obligations in 2009 to 12 percent in 2012.

Between 2011 and 2012, the share of PAMS contract obligations awarded under fixed price contract types grew from 43 percent to 47 percent, while cost reimbursement contract types declined from 42 percent to 40 percent.

Vehicle

In the 2009–2012 period, PAMS contract obligations awarded under single-award IDCs (-10.3 percent 3-year CAGRs) and purchase orders (-8.7 percent 3-year CAGRs) declined significantly faster than did overall PAMS contract obligations. Definitive contracts (-2.5 percent 3-year CAGR) declined at a rate comparable to overall PAMS contract obligations, while multiple-award IDCs (1.1 percent 3-year CAGR) and FSS and other IDVs (1.7 percent 3-year CAGR) showed slight growth. PAMS contract obligations coded as unlabeled IDVs have actually increased over the period (7.7 percent 3-year CAGR).

Between 2011 and 2012, the share of PAMS contract obligations awarded under definitive contracts increased from 26 percent to 28 percent. All other categories either held steady or saw only slight increases or decreases as a share of overall PAMS contract obligations.

Vendor Size

Between 2009 and 2012, PAMS contract obligations awarded to both small vendors (-0.4 percent 3-year CAGR) and medium vendors (-0.7 percent 3-year CAGR) held steady as overall PAMS contract obligations declined. PAMS contract obligations awarded to the Big 6 declined at a rate similar to that of overall PAMS contract obligations (-4.3 percent 3-year CAGR). Contract obligations awarded to large vendors declined at over twice the rate of overall PAMS contract obligations (-7.8 percent 3-year CAGR).

Between 2011 and 2012, the share of PAMS contract obligations awarded to medium vendors increased from 32 percent to 34 percent, and the share awarded to the Big 6 rose from 12 percent to 13 percent. The share awarded to small firms increased from 22 percent in 2011 to 23 percent in 2012, while the share awarded to large firms declined from 35 percent to 30 percent. Contract obligations awarded to large vendors declined by 21 percent, almost three times the rate of decline for overall PAMS contract obligations. Small vendors (-3 percent) and medium vendors (-1 percent) saw declines significantly smaller than that of overall PAMS contract obligations, while contract obligations for the Big 6 grew by 4 percent.

Top 10

The composition (if not the ordering) of the top 5 PAMS vendors held mostly steady between 2002 and 2012, with Raytheon (just outside the top 10 in 2012) replaced by Dyncorp International. There was more turnover in the rest of the top 10, with TRW (acquired by Northrop Grumman), Development Alternatives Group, and BAE Systems replaced by Fluor, L3 Communications, and CACI. The share of overall PAMS contract obligations awarded to the top 5 vendors fell from 18 percent in 2002 to 14 percent in 2012. The share awarded to the top 10 fell from 26 percent of contract obligations in 2002 to 24 percent in 2012. And as a share of the top 10, the share awarded to the top 5 vendors fell from 67 percent in 2002 to 60 percent in 2012.

The PAMS top 20 saw relatively minor shifts between 2011 and 2012. The most notable change was that Boeing, which was ranked 12th in PAMS in 2011, rose to 3rd in 2012, taking the place of Fluor (4th in 2011) in the top 5. Three companies outside the top 20 in 2011 rose into the top 20 in 2012: Mission Essential Personnel (22nd in 2011, 18th in 2012), MITRE (21st in 2011, 19th in 2012), and Deloitte (24th in 2011, 20th in 2012). No vendor within the top 20 in 2012 declined more three places from their 2011 ranking.

Figure 3-3: The Federal Research and Development Services Market, 2000–2012

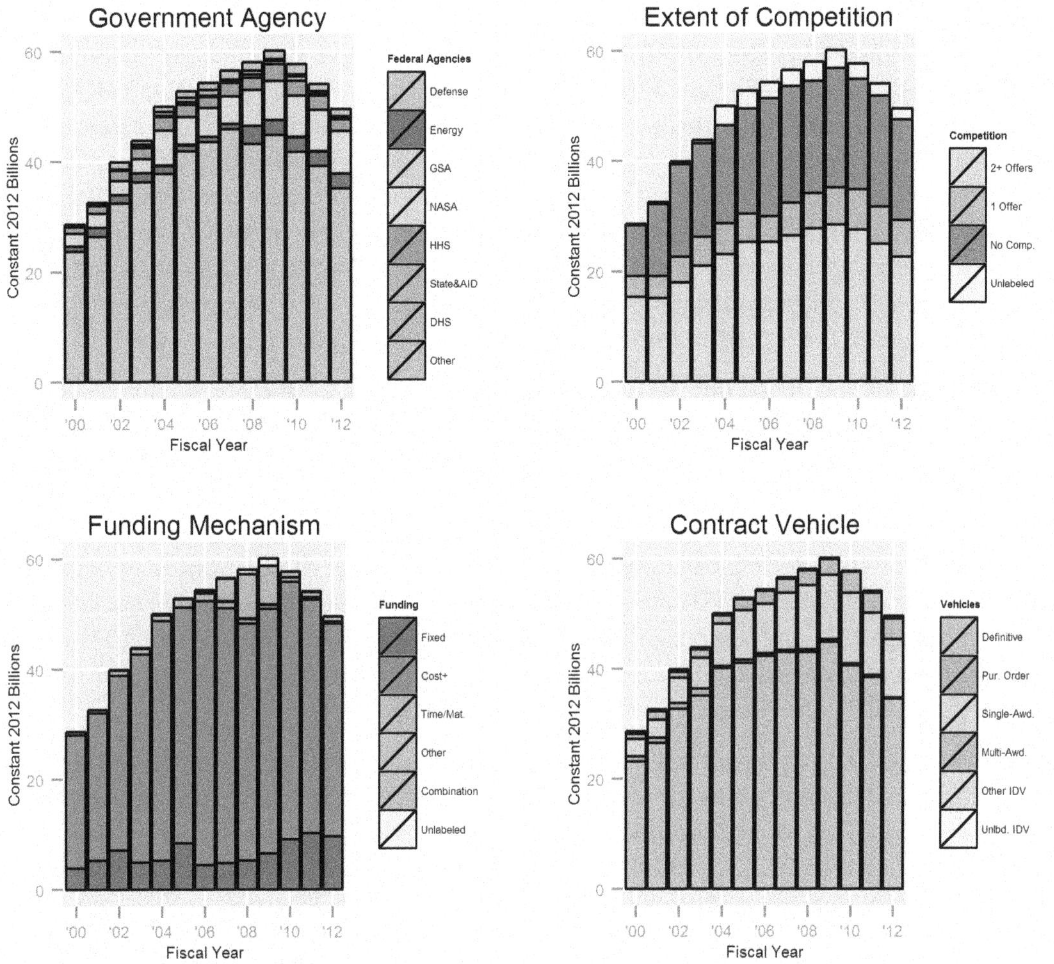

Top 10 Vendors

Vendor	2012 Millions	2011 Rank
Lockheed Martin	7,860	1
Boeing	4,340	2
Northrop Grumman	3,830	3
Raytheon	3,080	4
California Institute of Technology	1,680	5
Lawrence Livermore Nat'l Sec.*	1,640	6
United Technologies	1,290	8
Battelle	1,270	10
SAIC	1,170	13
General Dynamics	1,140	7
Top 10 R&D Obligations	33,840	
Total R&D Obligations	49,530	

* Joint Venture

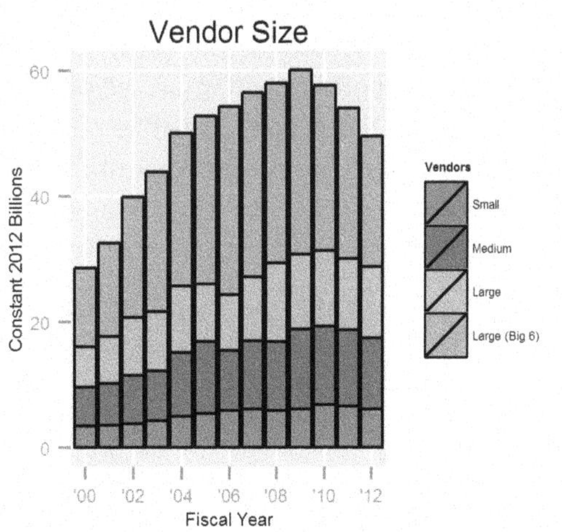

Source: FPDS; CSIS analysis.

R&D

From 2000 to 2012, DoD held large but declining majorities of R&D contract obligations, declining from 83 percent in 2002 to 71 percent in 2012, with NASA doubling from 8 percent in 2000 to 16 percent in 2012. Between 46 percent and 48 percent of R&D contract obligations were awarded after competition with multiple offers in most years, while over a third of contract obligations have been awarded without competition throughout the period. Over three quarters of R&D contract obligations were awarded under cost reimbursement contract types in most years, with fixed price approaching 20 percent in the early 2000s and in recent years. Over 80 percent of contract obligations were awarded under definitive contracts in the early 2000s, but that share has dropped to around 70 percent in recent years, with single-award IDCs rising from 11 percent in 2000 to 21 percent in 2012. The Big 6 have consistently captured around half of R&D contract obligations with other large and medium vendors capturing roughly equal share (around 20 percent), and small businesses holding steady in the low teens.

In the 2009–2012 period, R&D contract obligations declined at a -6.2 percent 3-year CAGR. Between 2011 and 2012, R&D contract obligations declined by 8 percent.

Government Agency

In the 2009–2012 period, R&D contract obligations for State/USAID (-26.8 percent 3-year CAGR) and HHS (-10.7 percent 3-year CAGR) declined sharply, at rates higher than that of R&D contract obligations overall. Defense (-7.9 percent 3-year CAGR) and other agencies (-5.0 percent 3-year CAGR) declined at rates comparable to overall R&D contract obligations. Four agencies saw minor growth in R&D contract obligations, despite the overall decline: DoE (0.2 percent 3-year CAGR), DHS (1.2 percent 3-year CAGR), GSA (2.5 percent 3-year CAGR), and NASA (3.1 percent 3-year CAGR).

Between 2011 and 2012, DHS contract obligations for R&D dropped by 29 percent, while HHS declined by 17 percent and State/USAID by 16 percent. DoD contract obligations for R&D declined by 10 percent. GSA contract obligations for R&D declined by 63 percent, though GSA accounted for only $150 million in R&D contract obligations in 2011. Other agencies held steady, while NASA (2 percent increase) and DoE (6 percent increase) saw growth between 2011 and 2012.

Competition

In the 2009–2012 period, R&D contract obligations awarded after competition with multiple offers declined moderately (-7.3 percent 3-year CAGR). In contrast to the trend in overall R&D contract obligations, both full competition with multiple offers and limited competition with multiple offers experienced declines, likely due to the relative rarity of multiple-award vehicles in R&D contracting. Contract obligations awarded without competition declined at a -5.6 percent 3-year CAGR, while contract obligations awarded after competition with a single offer were mostly stable (-0.5 percent 3-year CAGR).

Between 2011 and 2012, the shares of R&D contract obligations awarded after competition with multiple offers (46 percent) and without competition (37 percent) were unchanged. Competition with a single offer increased from 12 percent of R&D obligations to 13 percent of obligations.

Funding Mechanism

In the 2009–2012 period, R&D contract obligations awarded under fixed price contract types grew at a strong 14.2 percent 3-year CAGR, rising from 11 percent of contract obligations in 2009 to 20 percent in 2012, largely as the result of better data labeling. Contract obligations awarded under cost reimbursement contract types declined at a -4.6 percent 3-year CAGR, rising from 74 percent of contract obligations in 2009 to 78 percent in 2012. Contract obligations awarded under time and materials contract types declined at a -19.7 percent 3-year CAGR, but did not exceed 1 percent of R&D contract obligations during the period. Contract obligations awarded under combination contracts declined sharply (-50.0 percent 3-year CAGR), dropping from 12 percent of R&D contract obligations in 2009 to 2 percent in the years since.

Between 2011 and 2012, there was a slight increase in the share of contract obligations awarded under fixed price contract types (from 19 percent to 20 percent). All other categories were unchanged.

Vehicle

In the 2009–2012 period, R&D contract obligations awarded under definitive contracts declined at a -8.4 percent 3-year CAGR, dropping from 75 percent of contract obligations in 2009 to 70 percent in 2000. Single-award IDCs declined at a -3.0 percent 3-year CAGR, but rose from 19 percent of R&D contract obligations in 2009 to 21 percent in 2012. Contract obligations awarded under multiple-award IDCs grew at a 7.5 percent 3-year CAGR, rising from 5 percent of R&D contract obligations in 2009 to 7 percent in 2012. Purchase orders declined at a -11.6 percent 3-year CAGR, while FSS and other IDVs increased at a 54.8 percent 3-year CAGR, though neither exceeded $500 million in contract obligations between 2009 and 2012.

Between 2011 and 2012, there were no significant changes in the shares of R&D contract obligations awarded under the various vehicle types.

Vendor Size

In the 2009–2012 period, R&D contract obligations awarded to small vendors remained static (0.0 percent 3-year CAGR) as overall R&D contract obligations decreased. Contract obligations awarded to large contracts decreased more slowly than did overall R&D (-1.3 percent 3-year CAGR), while medium vendors declined at a rate similar to overall R&D (-4.0 percent 3-year CAGR). Contract obligations awarded to the Big 6 declined at nearly twice the rate of overall R&D (-11.0 percent 3-year CAGR).

Between 2011 and 2012, the share of contract obligations awarded to the Big 6 declined from 44 percent to 42 percent. The shares of R&D contract obligations awarded to small vendors (12 percent to 13 percent), medium vendors (22 percent to 23 percent), and large vendors (21 percent to 23 percent) all increased between 2011 and 2012. R&D contract obligations awarded to small vendors (-6 percent) and medium vendors (-7 percent) declined similarly to overall R&D, while the Big 6 declined sharply (-14 percent) and large vendors actually increased by 1 percent from 2011 to 2012.

Top 10

The top 5 vendors in R&D saw some turnover between 2002 and 2012, with General Dynamics and United Technologies falling out of the top 5 in 2012 (though both still in the top 10), replaced by Raytheon and the California Institute of Technology. The rest of the top 10 also saw changes: TRW and a Boeing/UTC joint venture fell out of the top 10, SAIC moved up into the top 10, and the Lawrence Livermore National Security joint venture took over management of the eponymous nuclear research facility from the University of California, placing 6th in 2012. The share of overall R&D contract obligations awarded to the top 5 vendors fell from 47 percent in 2002 to 42 percent in 2012, while the share awarded to the top 10 fell from 59 percent to 55 percent.

The top 5 R&D vendors remained the same, in the same order, between 2011 and 2012, and there were relatively minor changes through the rest of the top 20. Two companies rose from outside the top 20 in 2011: Roscosmos (21st in 2011, 16th in 2012) and MITRE (22nd in 2011, 18th in 2012). The largest-ranking decline was for ATK, which fell from 15th in 2011 to 20th in 2012.

Figure 3-4: The Federal Equipment-Related Services Market, 2000–2012

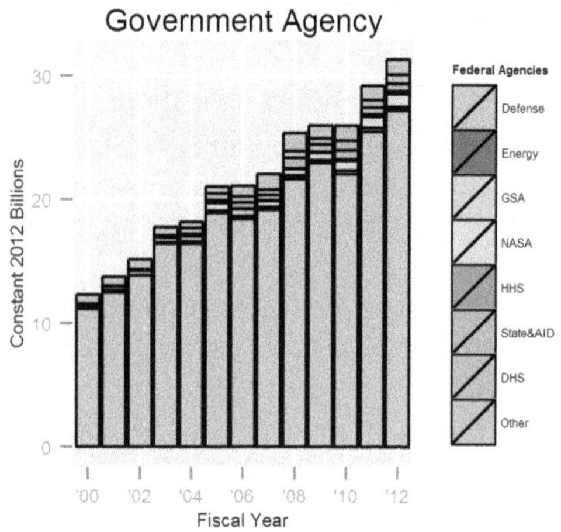

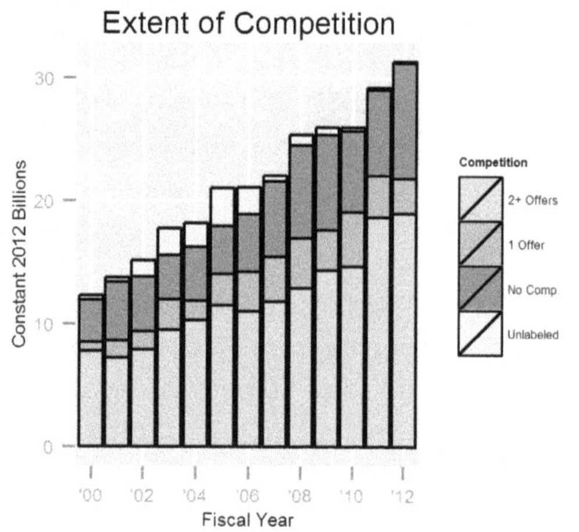

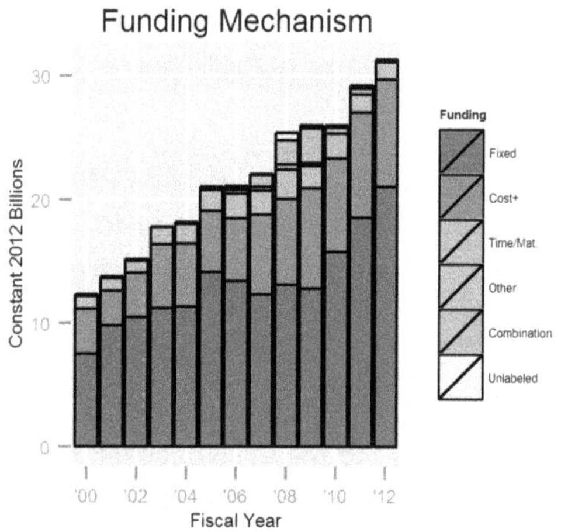

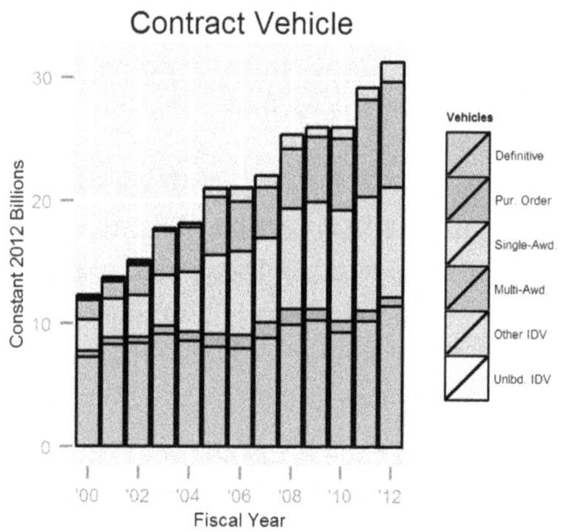

Top 10 Vendors

Vendor	2012 Millions	2011 Rank
Boeing	2,800	11
L3 Communications	1,760	3
Lockheed Martin	1,670	1
Raytheon	1,550	2
AP Moller Maersk	1,250	9
BAE Systems	1,110	5
FedEx	1,040	7
Northrop Grumman	1,020	4
Dyncorp International	950	8
General Dynamics	810	6
Top 10 ERS Obligations	18,070	
Total ERS Obligations	31,330	

* Joint Venture

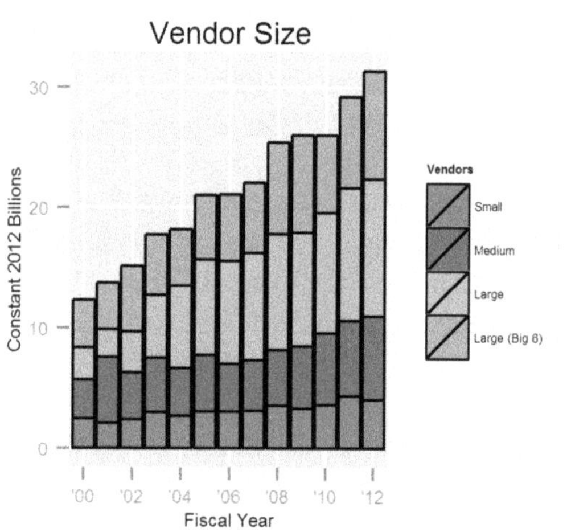

Source: FPDS; CSIS analysis.

ERS

From 2000 to 2012, DoD accounted for 85 percent or more of ERS contract obligations in every year, while no other single agency accounted for more than 3 percent in any given year. Over half of ERS contract obligations have been awarded after competition with multiple offers throughout the period observed, though the precise shares have fluctuated significantly. Over 60 percent of ERS contract obligations were awarded under fixed price contract types though most of the period observed, except for 2007–2009, when combination contracts grew more common. Over 50 percent of ERS contract obligations were awarded under definitive contract types from 2000 to 2003, but definitive contracts have not exceeded 40 percent since 2004; contract obligations awarded under single-award IDCs and multiple-award IDCs have grown through most of the period observed. And since 2003, the largest share of ERS contract obligations (between 36 percent and 41 percent) have been awarded to large vendors.

In the 2009–2012 period, ERS contract obligations grew at a 6.4 percent 3-year CAGR, making ERS the only service area that saw growth in this period. Between 2011 and 2012, overall ERS contract obligations grew by 7 percent.

Government Agency

In the 2009–2012 period, ERS contract obligations by DoD grew at a 5.8 percent 3-year CAGR. Given that DoD accounted for over 85 percent of ERS contract obligations from 2009 to 2012, it is not surprising that the rate of growth for ERS within DoD tracks closely to the overall rate of growth for ERS contract obligations. Several other agencies saw strong growth in ERS contract obligations, but only DHS (14.9 percent 3-year CAGR) and NASA (19.6 percent 3-year CAGR) exceeded $600 million in ERS contract obligations during the period.

Between 2011 and 2012, DoD, NASA, and State/USAID contract obligations for ERS grew at the same rate (7 percent) as overall ERS contract obligations. A few agencies, including DHS (24 percent growth), saw growth rates significantly faster than that of overall ERS contract obligations.

Competition

In the 2009–2012 period, ERS contract obligations awarded after competition with multiple offers grew faster than overall ERS contract obligations (9.7 percent 3-year CAGR) , driven by strong growth in limited competition with multiple offers (16.1 percent 3-year CAGR). The share of contract obligations awarded after competition with multiple offers grew from 55 percent in 2009 to 61 percent in 2012, but limited competition with multiple offers accounted for almost half of overall competition with multiple offers in 2012. Contract obligations awarded without competition grew at a rate similar to overall ERS contract obligations (6.7 percent 3-year CAGR), dropping as a share of overall ERS contract obligations from 30 percent in 2009 to 24 percent in 2011, before rebounding in 2012. Contract obligations awarded after competition with a single offer declined at a -4.5 percent 3-year CAGR, falling as a share of ERS contract obligations from 13 percent in 2009 to 9 percent in 2012. Unlabeled has continued to decline in ERS contract obligations (-40.9 percent 3-year CAGR).

Between 2011 and 2012, the share of ERS contract obligations awarded after competition with multiple offers declined from 64 percent to 61 percent, while the share awarded without competition rose from 24 percent to 30 percent. The share of contract obligations awarded after competition with a single offer declined from 12 percent in 2011 to 9 percent in 2012.

Funding Mechanism

In the 2009–2012 period, ERS contract obligations awarded under fixed price contract types grew at a robust 18.1 percent 3-year CAGR, rising from 49 percent of ERS contract obligations in 2009 to 67 percent in 2012. Contract obligations awarded under cost reimbursement contract types grew more slowly than overall ERS contract obligations (2.1 percent 3-year CAGR), and fell from 31 percent of ERS contract obligations to 28 percent in 2012. Time and materials contracts declined moderately (-7.5 percent 3-year CAGR), falling from 7 percent of ERS contract obligations in 2009 to 5 percent in 2012. Combination contracts, which accounted for 11 percent of ERS contract obligations in 2009, declined sharply to less than 1 percent in 2010 and every year since.

Between 2011 and 2012, the share of ERS contract obligations awarded under fixed price contract types increased from 63 percent to 67 percent, while the share awarded under cost reimbursement contract types declined from 29 percent to 28 percent. The share awarded under time and materials contract types held steady at 5 percent.

Vehicle

In the 2009–2012 period, ERS contract obligations awarded under definitive contracts grew more slowly than overall ERS contract obligations (3.7 percent 3-year CAGR). Purchase orders declined sharply (-8.5 percent 3-year CAGR), while single-award IDCs were stagnant (0.7 percent 3-year CAGR) and multiple-award IDCs grew at nearly three times the rate of overall ERS contract obligations (17.6 percent 3-year CAGR). FSS and other IDVs grew at nearly five times the rate of overall ERS contract obligations (29.4 percent 3-year CAGR).

Between 2011 and 2012, the share of ERS contract obligations awarded under definitive contracts grew from 35 percent to 37 percent, while single-award IDCs declined from 32 percent to 29 percent. Multiple-award IDCs held steady at 27 percent, purchase orders declined from 3 percent to 2 percent, and FSS and other IDVs rose from 3 percent to 5 percent.

Vendor Size

In the 2009–2012 period, ERS contract obligations awarded to small vendors (6.6 percent 3-year CAGR) and large vendors (6.2 percent) grew at rates similar to the rate of growth for overall ERS contract obligations. Contract obligations awarded to medium vendors grew faster (10.7 percent 3-year CAGR), while growth for the Big 6 vendors lagged behind growth in overall ERS contract obligations (3.7 percent 3-year CAGR).

Between 2011 and 2012, the share of ERS contract obligations awarded to small vendors declined from 15 percent to 13 percent. Medium vendors saw a small increase, from 21 percent to 22 percent, while large vendors declined from 38 percent to 36 percent. The Big 6, meanwhile, rose from 26 percent to 29 percent, recovering some of the share they lost after 2009.

Top 10

There was significant turnover in the top 5 vendors for ERS between 2002 and 2012. Northrop Grumman, Dyncorp International, and General Dynamics fell out of the top 5 (but remained in the top 10 in 2012), replaced by Boeing, L3 Communications, and AP Moller Maersk. BAE Systems is the only other new vendor in the top 10 in 2012, while two of the top 10 vendors from 2002, North American Airlines (acquired by Global Aviation Holdings, which filed for Chapter 11 bankruptcy in 2012) and Southwest Marine, fell out of the top 10. As a share of overall ERS contract obligations, the top 5 vendors accounted for 40 percent in 2002, but only 29 percent in 2012, while the share awarded to the top 10 vendors declined from 53 percent in 2002 to 45 percent in 2012.

There was significant movement within the top 5 ERS vendors between 2011 and 2012, with Boeing rising from 11th in 2011 to 1st in 2012, and AP Moller Maersk rising from 9th in 2011 to 5th in 2012. Two companies outside the top 20 in 2011 rose into the top 20 in 2012: Global Aviation (outside the top

100 in 2011, 13th in 2012) and AC First, an AECOM/CACI joint venture (22nd in 2011, 14th in 2012). United Technologies saw the largest decline, from 13th in 2011 to 20th in 2012.

Figure 3-5: The Federal Facilities-Related Services and Construction Services Market, 2000–2012

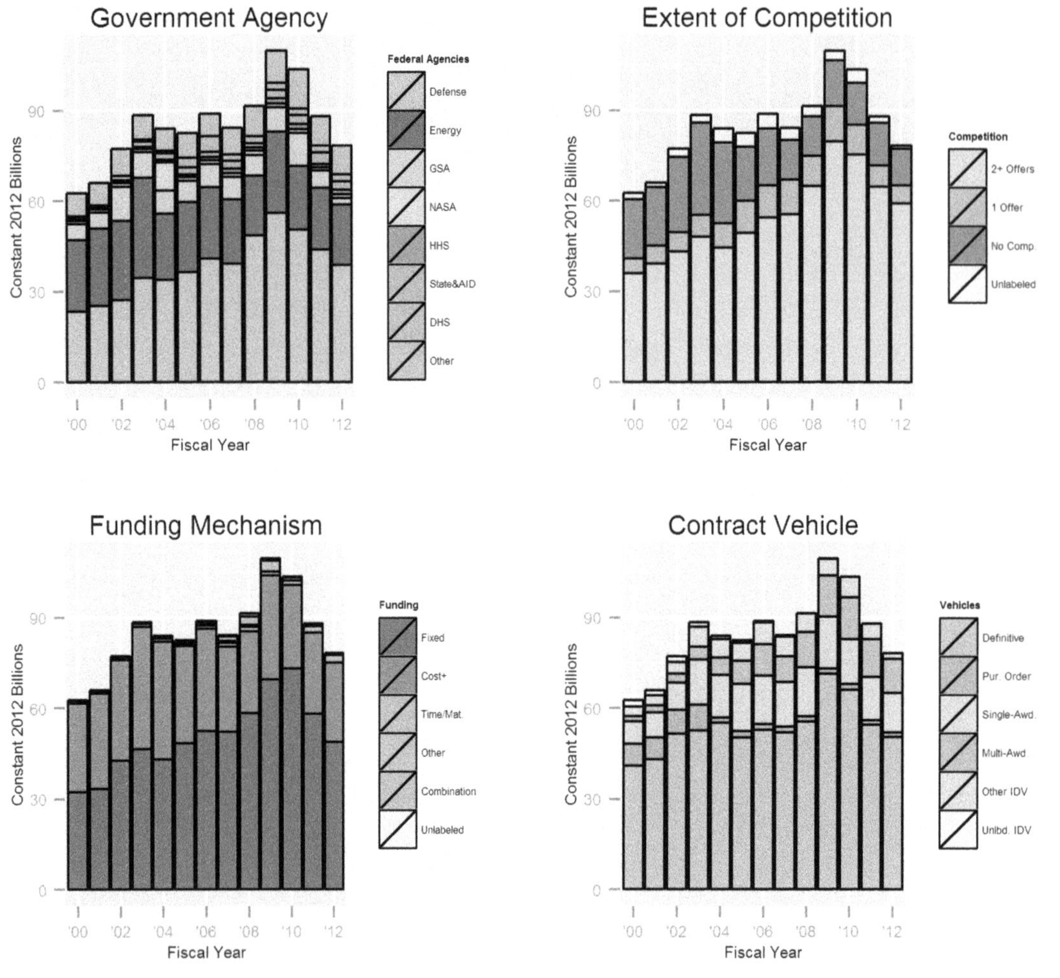

Top 10 Vendors

Vendor	2012 Millions	2011 Rank
Lockheed Martin	2,990	1
Los Alamos National Security*	2,150	2
Bechtel	2,110	3
URS	1,980	4
UT-Battelle Joint Venture*	1,250	5
McDermott International	1,010	10
Hensel Phelps	960	14
University of California	950	9
CH2M Hill	940	8
Battelle	830	7
Top 10 FRS&C Obligations	21,610	
Total FRS&C Obligations	78,360	

* Joint Venture

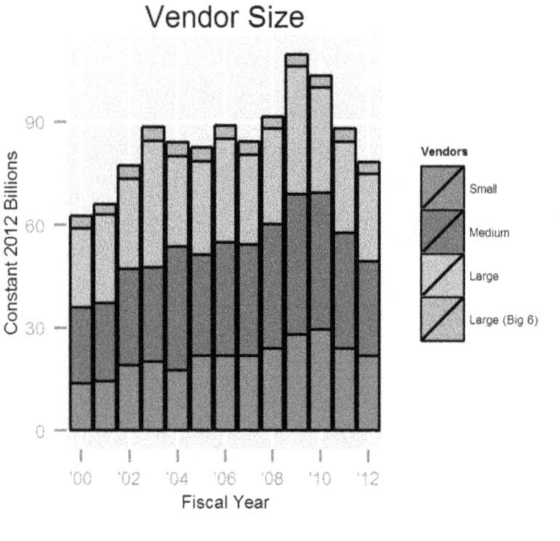

Source: FPDS; CSIS analysis.

FRS&C

From 2000 to 2012, a growing majority of FRS&C contract obligations were awarded by DoD, rising from 37 percent in 2000 to over 50 percent by the end of the period, with a significant (38 percent in 2000) but declining (25 percent or less since 2007) share awarded by DoE. Growing majorities of contract obligations have been awarded after competition with multiple offers, rising from 58 percent in 2000 to over 70 percent since 2008. Similarly, growing majorities of contract obligations have been awarded under fixed price contract types, rising from 52 percent in 2000 to a high of 71 percent in 2010, before declines in the last two years. Over 60 percent of contract obligations have been awarded under definitive contracts in every year but one during the period, while multiple-award IDCs have grown steadily through the period observed. Small, medium, and large vendors have all captured significant shares of FRS&C contract obligations throughout the period observed, while contract obligations awarded to the Big 6 vendors never exceeded 5 percent after 2000.

In the 2009–2012 period, FRS&C contract obligations declined at a -10.6 percent 3-year CAGR. Between 2011 and 2012, overall FRS&C contract obligations declined by 11 percent. **Both of these figures, and all of the analysis below, are distorted by the fact that GSA has almost entirely stopped reporting contracting for lease of office buildings (totaling $4.7 billion in 2010) into FPDS over the last two years. If this contracting activity were still in FPDS at approximately FY 2010 levels, it would represent nearly 5 percent of total FRS&C contract obligations.**

Note that FRS&C contract obligations were temporarily inflated in 2009 and 2010 due to the American Recovery and Reinvestment Act (ARRA) of 2009, which accounted for 12 percent of FRS&C contract obligations in 2009 and 2010. See Chapter 5 for further discussion of the impact of ARRA on services contract trends.

Government Agency

In the 2009–2012 period, DoD contract obligations for FRS&C declined at a similar rate to overall FRS&C contract obligations (-11.4 percent 3-year CAGR), as did DoE (-9.7 percent 3-year CAGR). Most other agencies saw much slower declines: NASA (-3.3 percent 3-year CAGR), other agencies (-2.9 percent 3-year CAGR), HHS (-1.5 percent 3-year CAGR), DHS (-0.9 percent 3-year CAGR), and State/USAID (-0.7 percent 3-year CAGR). GSA declined at a -34.4 percent 3-year CAGR, but most of that decline is due to GSA no longer reporting much of its FRS&C contracting inventory into FPDS.

Between 2011 and 2012, FRS&C contract obligations by State/USAID (-27 percent) and GSA (-60 percent) declined faster than overall FRS&C contract obligations, though the change for GSA is a reporting issue rather than a change in contracting trends. DoD (-12 percent) declined at a rate similar to that of overall FRS&C contract obligations. DHS (-7 percent) and DoE (-2 percent) declined more slowly than overall FRS&C, other agencies were stagnant (0 percent), and NASA (10 percent) and HHS (47 percent) saw significant growth between 2011 and 2012.

Competition

In the 2009–2012 period, FRS&C contract obligations awarded after competition with multiple offers declined at a rate similar to that of overall FRS&C contract obligations (-9.5 percent 3-year CAGR), but increased as a share of FRS&C contract obligations from 73 percent in 2009 to 75 percent in 2012. As with many of the other service areas, full competition with multiple offers (-13.1 percent 3-year CAGR) declined more rapidly than limited competition with multiple offers (-0.7 percent 3-year CAGR). Contract obligations awarded without competition declined more slowly than overall FRS&C contract obligations (-6.6 percent 3-year CAGR), and rose from 14 percent of contract obligations in 2009 to 15 percent in 2012. Contract obligations awarded after competition with a single offer declined sharply (-19.9 percent

3-year CAGR), falling from 11 percent of FRS&C contract obligations in 2009 to 8 percent in 2012. And unlabeled contracts have continued their decline, from 3 percent in 2009 to 1 percent in 2012.

Between 2011 and 2012, the share of FRS&C contract obligations awarded after competition with multiple offers increased from 74 percent to 75 percent, while the share awarded without competition declined from 16 percent to 15 percent. The share of contract obligations awarded after competition with a single offer held steady at 8 percent.

Funding Mechanism

In the 2009–2012 period, FRS&C contract obligations awarded under fixed price contract types declined at a rate similar to that of overall FRS&C contract obligations (-11.2 percent 3-year CAGR). Contract obligations awarded under cost reimbursement contract types fell more slowly than overall FRS&C contract obligations (-8.4 percent 3-year CAGR). Contract obligations awarded under time and materials contracts grew rapidly (24.3 percent 3-year CAGR), while combination contracts and unlabeled contracts are no longer significant factors.

Between 2011 and 2012, the share of FRS&C contract obligations awarded under fixed price contract types declined from 66 percent to 62 percent, while the share awarded under cost reimbursement contract types grew from 31 percent to 34 percent.

Vehicle

In the 2009–2012 period, FRS&C contract obligations awarded under definitive contracts declined at a rate similar to overall FRS&C contract obligations (-10.9 percent 3-year CAGR). Contract obligations awarded under single-award IDCs (-8.2 percent 3-year CAGR), purchase orders (-6.9 percent 3-year CAGR), and multiple-award IDCs (-6.8 percent 3-year CAGR) all declined more slowly than overall FRS&C contract obligations. FSS and other IDVs declined nearly three times as fast as overall FRS&C contract obligations (-28.8 percent 3-year CAGR).

Between 2011 and 2012, the share of FRS&C contract obligations awarded under definitive contracts increased from 62 percent to 64 percent, single-award IDCs increased from 16 percent to 17 percent, and FSS and other IDVs declined from 6 percent to 3 percent. Purchase orders and multiple-award IDCs held steady at 2 percent and 14 percent, respectively.

Vendor Size

In the 2009–2012 period, FRS&C contract obligations awarded to large vendors declined at a rate similar to that of overall FRS&C contract obligations (-11.9 percent 3-year CAGR). Medium vendors declined slightly faster (-12.5 percent 3-year CAGR), while small vendors declined slightly less steeply (-7.9 percent 3-year CAGR). The Big 6 vendors, by contrast, actually saw slight growth (1.7 percent 3-year CAGR) during the period.

Between 2011 and 2012, FRS&C contract obligations awarded to small vendors declined more slowly than overall FRS&C contract obligations (-9 percent), but increased as a share of contract obligations from 27 percent to 28 percent. Large vendors and the Big 6 vendors both saw smaller declines (-4 percent), and both increased as a share of overall FRS&C contract obligations: large vendors rose from 30 percent to 32 percent, and the Big 6 rose from 4 percent to 5 percent. Contract obligations awarded to medium vendors declined by 19 percent, falling as a share of overall FRS&C contract obligations from 38 percent to 35 percent.

Top 10

There was significant turnover in the top 5 for FRS&C between 2002 and 2012, with the University of California (which remained in the top 10 in 2012), Association of Service Disabled Veterans, and Acepex Management falling out, replaced by the Los Alamos National Security joint venture, URS, and the UT-Battelle joint venture to manage Oak Ridge National Laboratory. There was similar turnover in the rest of the top 10, with the Washington Savannah River Company joint venture (replaced by the Savannah River Nuclear Solutions joint venture, just outside the top 10 in 2012), University of Chicago, and Fluor falling out of the top 10. In 2012, the new companies in the top 10 are Hensel Philipps, CH2M Hill, and Battelle. As a share of overall FRS&C contract obligations, the top 5 vendors declined from 27 percent in 2002 to 13 percent in 2012, the lowest of any service area. The top 10 declined as a share of overall FRS&C contract obligations from 35 percent in 2002 to 19 percent in 2012, also the lowest of any service area.

The top five FRS&C vendors were unchanged between 2011 and 2012, but there was significant change in the rest of the top 20. Four companies rose into the top 20 in 2012: SAIC (22nd in 2011, 14th in 2012), PCCP Constructors joint venture (outside the top 100 in 2011, 16th in 2012), Babcock & Wilcox (21st in 2011, 18th in 2012), and the Kiewet-Turner joint venture (outside the top 100 in 2011, 19th in 2012). Three other companies saw significant rankings rises: McDermott International (10th in 2011, 6th in 2012), Hensel Phelps (14th in 2011, 7th in 2012), and Honeywell (17th in 2011, 13th in 2012). The biggest decline was for ITT, which fell from 6th in 2011 to 17th in 2012, in large part due to a spinoff of their defense technology business in October 2011.

Figure 3-6: The Federal Medical Services Market, 2000–2012

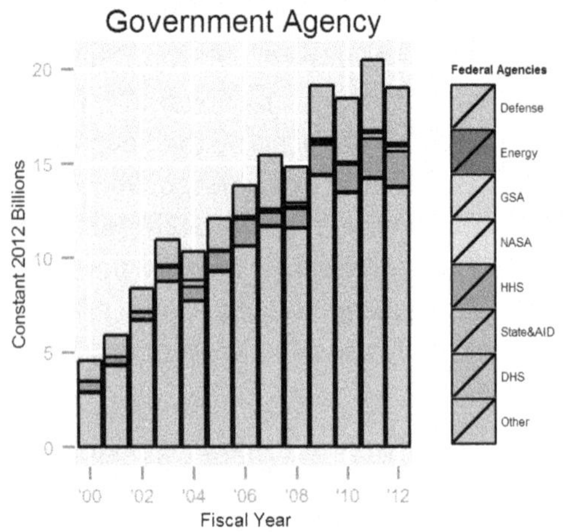

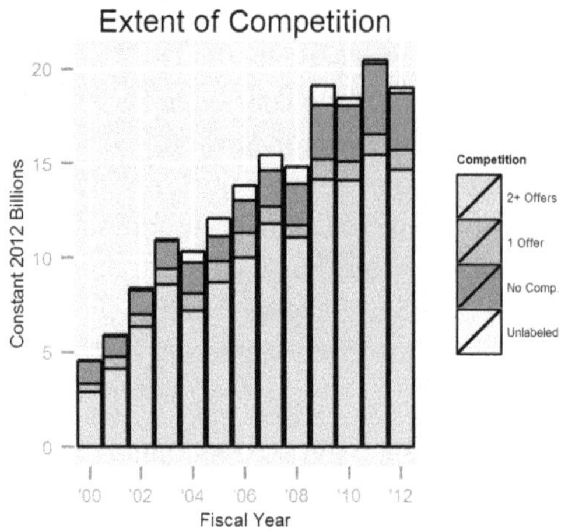

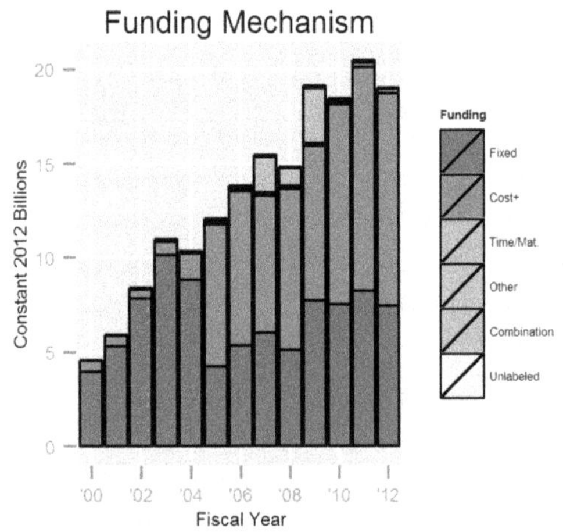

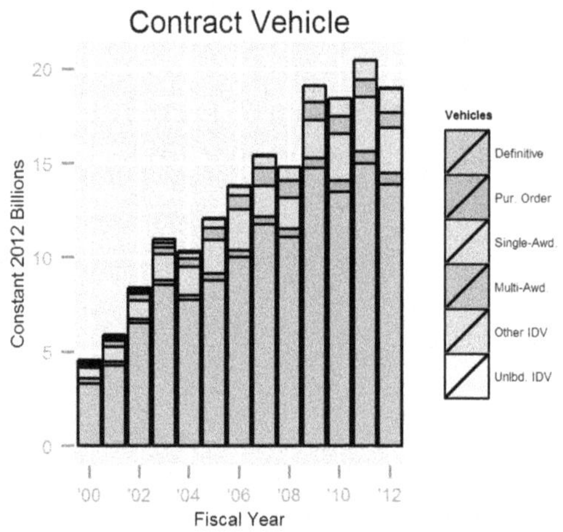

Top 10 Vendors

Vendor	2012 Millions	2011 Rank
Humana	3,470	1
TriWest Healthcare	3,010	2
Health Net	2,940	3
Highmark	550	4
Express Scripts	480	5
Johns Hopkins APL	310	7
Martin's Point Health Care	280	8
LHI	280	10
Blue Cross & Blue Shield	190	11
Qtc Management	170	13
Top 10 MED Obligations	13,010	
Total MED Obligations	19,010	

* Joint Venture

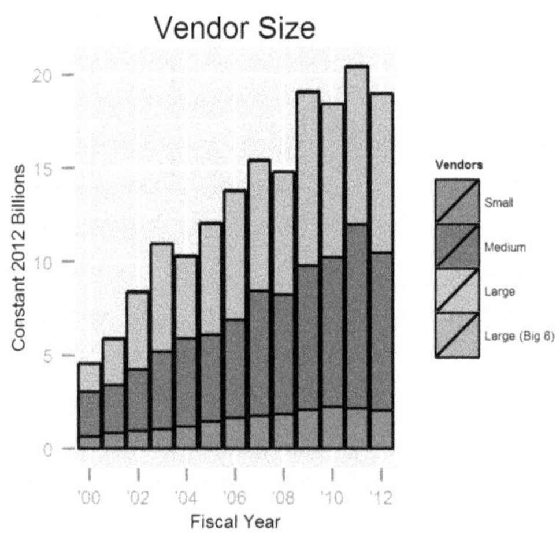

Source: FPDS; CSIS analysis.

MED

From 2000 to 2012, DoD has accounted for 70 percent or more of MED contract obligations in most years. HHS is the only other single agency that has exceeded 4 percent in any given year, rising as high as 11 percent in 2000. Nearly three quarters of MED contract obligations have been awarded after competition with multiple offers in most years during the period observed. Over 85 percent of MED contract obligations were awarded under fixed price contract types from 2000 to 2004, but since then, half or more of contract obligations have been awarded under cost reimbursement contract types in most years. Nearly three-quarters of contract obligations have been awarded under definitive contracts in every year during the period observed. And MED contract obligations have been relatively evenly split between medium and large firms, with around 10 percent awarded to small firms and 1 percent or less awarded to the Big 6.

In the 2009–2012 period, MED contract obligations declined at a -0.2 percent 3-year CAGR. Between 2011 and 2012, MED contract obligations declined by 7 percent.

Government Agency

In the 2009–2012 period, MED contract obligations by DoD declined at a -1.5 percent 3-year CAGR, comparable to the overall rate of decline for MED contract obligations. HHS contract obligations increased at a 5.5 percent 3-year CAGR, while other agencies increased at a 1.8 percent 3-year CAGR. No other single agency accounted for more than $300 million in MED contract obligations during this period.

Between 2011 and 2012, MED contract obligations for DoD decreased by 3 percent, less than half the overall rate of decline for MED. HHS MED contract obligations declined by 11 percent, while MED contract obligations by other agencies decreased by 20 percent

Competition

In the 2009–2012 period, MED contract obligations awarded after competition with multiple offers increased slightly (1.3 percent 3-year CAGR), though most of the increase was in limited competition with multiple offers (15.8 percent 3-year CAGR) rather than full competition with multiple offers (0.1 percent 3-year CAGR). MED contract obligations awarded without competition grew at a 1 percent 3-year CAGR, while contract obligations awarded after competition with a single offer were stagnant (-0.1 percent 3-year CAGR).

Between 2011 and 2012, the share of contract obligations awarded after competition with multiple offers increased from 75 percent to 77 percent, while the share awarded without competition fell from 18 percent to 16 percent. Contract obligations awarded after competition with a single offer held steady at 6 percent.

Funding Mechanism

In the 2009–2012 period, MED contract obligations awarded under fixed price contract types declined at a -1.2 percent 3-year CAGR, hovering between 39 percent and 41 percent of overall MED contract obligations. Contract obligations awarded under cost reimbursement contract types have grown strongly (11.0 percent 3-year CAGR), rising from 43 percent of MED contract obligations in 2009 to 59 percent in 2012. Much of that growth came as the result of a decline in combination contracts, which dropped from 15 percent of MED contract obligations in 2009 to less than 1 percent in every year since. Time and materials contracts have grown at a robust 27.0 percent 3-year CAGR, but did not exceed $250 million during the period.

Between 2011 and 2012, the share of MED contract obligations awarded under fixed price contract types declined from 40 percent to 39 percent, while the share awarded under cost reimbursement contract types increased from 58 percent to 59 percent.

Vehicle

In the 2009–2012 period, MED contract obligations awarded under definitive contracts declined slightly faster than overall MED contract obligations (-2.0 percent 3-year CAGR). Purchase orders (3.3 percent 3-year CAGR) and single-award IDCs (6.9 percent 3-year CAGR) both saw growth during the period, while multiple-award IDCs (-7.0 percent 3-year CAGR) declined several times faster than overall MED contract obligations. Contract obligations for FSS and other IDVs grew at a 14.2 percent 3-year CAGR.

Between 2011 and 2012, the share of MED contract obligations awarded under definitive contracts and purchase orders held steady at 73 percent and 3 percent, respectively. Single-award IDCs declined from 14 percent to 13 percent, while multiple-award IDCs declined from 5 percent to 4 percent. FSS and other IDVs were the only vehicle category to see growth in share, from 5 percent to 7 percent.

Vendors Size

In the 2009–2012 period, MED contract obligations awarded to small vendors declined at the same rate as overall MED contract obligations (0.2 percent 3-year CAGR). Contract obligations awarded to medium vendors grew at a 3.1 percent 3-year CAGR. Large vendors saw a mild decline (-3.0 percent 3-year CAGR), while the Big 6 were awarded less than $50 million in every year during the period.

Between 2011 and 2012, MED contract obligations awarded to small vendors declined by 5 percent, holding steady as a share of overall MED contract obligations at 11 percent. Contract obligations awarded to medium vendors declined by 14 percent, declining as a share of overall MED contract obligations from 48 percent to 44 percent. Contract obligations awarded to large vendors grew by 1 percent, rising as a share of overall MED contract obligations from 41 percent to 45 percent.

Top 10

There was moderate turnover in the top 5 MED vendors between 2002 and 2012. Sierra Military Health Service and the Johns Hopkins Applied Physics Laboratory (which fell just outside the top 5 in 2012) dropped out, replaced by Highmark and Express Scripts. There was significant turnover in the rest of the top 10, with SAIC, Christus Health (which fell just outside the top 10 in 2012), and CR Associates replaced by LHI, Blue Cross & Blue Shield, and QTC Management. The top 5 accounted for 64 percent share of overall MED contract obligations in 2002, compared to 55 percent in 2012. The top 10 vendors accounted for a 70 percent share of overall MED contract obligations in 2002, compared to 61 percent in 2012.

The top 5 MED vendors were unchanged between 2011 and 2012, and there was only minor movement in the rest of the top 10. Outside of the top 10, the total dollar figures for companies are well below CSIS's investigation thresholds, and as such the data lacks sufficient precision to do meaningful trend analysis.

Cross-Area Participation by Vendors

Table 3-1: Cross-Area Participation by Vendors, 2002 and 2012

2002	ICT	PAMS	R&D	ERS	FRS&C	MED
ICT	100%	33%	12%	9%	10%	2%
PAMS	8%	100%	8%	5%	10%	2%
R&D	12%	35%	100%	6%	8%	3%
ERS	6%	14%	4%	100%	18%	1%
FRS&C	2%	8%	2%	5%	100%	1%
MED	2%	6%	2%	1%	3%	100%

2012	ICT	PAMS	R&D	ERS	FRS&C	MED
ICT	100%	41%	9%	16%	12%	4%
PAMS	8%	100%	5%	8%	10%	4%
R&D	12%	33%	100%	10%	12%	7%
ERS	8%	19%	4%	100%	18%	3%
FRS&C	4%	15%	3%	11%	100%	2%
MED	3%	16%	4%	5%	5%	100%

Source: FPDS; CSIS analysis.

Many of the vendors that are active in the federal services market provide the government with services in more than one area. Table 3-2 shows the cross-area participation of the vendors in the federal services industrial base. The most common area of cross-participation is with PAMS: the highest percentages of cross participation for vendors in every service area are with PAMS, and with the exception of R&D, this cross-participation has increased over the past decade. This relationship is primarily unidirectional, as PAMS vendors only reach double-digit cross participation in FRS&C. Another notable trend is the slight rise across all service areas in cross-participation into ERS and MED contracting, though the percentages for MED are still quite low.

Cross-Area Participation by the Overall Top 20 Federal Services Vendors

Table 3-2: Cross-Area Participation by the Overall Top 20 Federal Services Vendors, 2002

	Vendor	PAMS	ICT	R&D	FRS&C	ERS	MED	Total
1	Lockheed Martin	2,430	1,590	7,340	2,800	840	0	15,000
2	University of California	40	-	640	8,830	-	0	9,510
3	Boeing	1,830	10	5,820	20	370	-	8,050
4	Northrop Grumman	1,320	1,160	1,690	80	1,760	0	6,020
5	Raytheon	1,450	420	1,550	360	1,550	0	5,320
Subtotal for Top 5	-	**7,060**	**3,180**	**17,040**	**12,100**	**4,520**	**10**	**43,910**
6	General Dynamics	380	780	2,440	200	830	-	4,630
7	Bechtel	210	-	10	4,020	-	-	4,230
8	SAIC	1,550	1,440	590	60	130	130	3,900
9	ASDV	-	-	-	2,980	-	-	2,980
10	Dyncorp International	530	650	170	280	1,010	0	2,640
11	TRW	1,270	350	770	210	10	-	2,610
12	Computer Sciences Corp.	620	1,440	290	140	10	0	2,500
13	Health Net	0	-	-	0	-	2,120	2,120
14	BAE Systems	660	540	250	400	100	10	1,960
15	Acepex Management	-	-	-	1,850	0	-	1,850
16	United Technologies	20	0	1,600	0	150	-	1,780
17	Washington Savannah River Company*	0	-	-	1,780	-	-	1,780
18	Humana	-	-	-	-	-	1,630	1,630
19	Booz Allen Hamilton	620	560	190	30	-	0	1,400
20	Electronic Data Systems	100	1,210	10	0	-	0	1,340
Total for Top 20	-	**13,030**	**10,140**	**23,360**	**24,040**	**6,770**	**3,910**	**81,250**
Total for all industry	-	**48,670**	**25,570**	**39,840**	**77,270**	**15,130**	**8,380**	**214,880**

* Joint Venture

Source: FPDS; CSIS analysis. All figures in 2012 millions.

Table 3-3: Cross-Area Participation by the Overall Top 20 Federal Services Vendors, 2012

	Vendor	PAMS	ICT	R&D	FRS&C	ERS	MED	Total
1	Lockheed Martin	3,500	1,960	7,860	2,990	1,670	0	17,970
2	Boeing	2,620	70	4,340	30	2,800	-	9,850
3	Northrop Grumman	2,850	1,430	3,830	130	1,020	0	9,260
4	SAIC	2,440	2,320	1,170	660	150	10	6,760
5	Raytheon	1,460	280	3,080	60	1,550	-	6,430
Subtotal for Top 5	-	**12,860**	**6,060**	**20,280**	**3,860**	**7,190**	**20**	**50,280**
6	General Dynamics	1,230	1,260	1,140	60	810	0	4,500
7	L3 Communications	1,680	370	500	30	1,760	0	4,350
8	Booz Allen Hamilton	2,180	690	1,130	20	0	30	4,040
9	Computer Sciences Corp.	1,820	1,370	60	250	390	0	3,900
10	Dyncorp International	2,220	0	30	300	950	40	3,540
11	Humana	0	0	-	-	-	3,470	3,470
12	URS	1,000	80	50	1,980	360	-	3,470
13	Bechtel	1,190	-	-	2,110	-	-	3,300
14	Health Net	200	-	0	-	-	2,940	3,140
15	BAE Systems	960	330	390	320	1,110	-	3,110
16	TriWest Healthcare	0	-	-	-	-	3,010	3,010
17	Battelle	140	0	1,270	830	40	0	2,290
18	CACI	1,500	520	250	0	0	0	2,270
19	Hewlett-Packard	230	1,940	50	0	0	-	2,220
20	ITT	680	360	370	600	200	-	2,200
Total for Top 20	-	**27,900**	**12,980**	**25,540**	**10,360**	**12,820**	**9,500**	**99,100**
Total for all industry	-	**96,250**	**33,270**	**49,530**	**78,360**	**31,330**	**19,010**	**307,750**

Source: FPDS; CSIS analysis. All figures in 2012 millions.

Between 2002 and 2012, the service area participation of the top 5 federal services vendors has diversified significantly. FRS&C contract obligations in the top 5 have dropped significantly, largely due to changes in contract awards for management of the national nuclear laboratories, but contract obligations in every other category except MED have increased significantly. It is notable that, unlike in 2002, every vendor in the top 5 in 2012 has been awarded over $1 billion in contract obligations in three or more service areas (compared to only three in 2002), showing the degree to which the biggest companies have diversified in order to maintain or increase their share of the federal services contracting market. Overall, the top 20 vendors have become more PAMS and ERS focused, while FRS&C obligations have been more highly distributed to smaller vendors. In fact, the share of total FRS&C contract obligations awarded to the top 20 vendors has declined from 31 percent in 2002 to 13 percent in 2012. Vendors providing MED services have become more significant factors in the top 20, but minimal MED contract obligations are awarded to top vendors that are not healthcare-focused firms.

Predictably, R&D is the most heavily concentrated service area, with the top 5 and top 20 accounted for 43 percent and 59 percent, respectively, of total R&D contract obligations in 2002. In 2012, the shares of R&D awarded to the top 5 (41 percent) and top 20 (52 percent) declined, but R&D remained the service area most heavily weighted to top vendors. The other four service areas (excluding FRS&C) saw minimal change in the share of overall contract obligations awarded to the top 20 between 2002 and 2012.

Chapter 4: Contracting for Services by Key Government Agencies

This chapter examines trends in service contracts for seven key government agencies: Department of Defense, Department of Energy, Department of Health and Human Services, Department of Homeland Security, General Services Administration, Department of State and USAID, and NASA, plus a category for all other agencies. For each, the analysis includes data on contract obligations by service area, the level of competition, and types of funding mechanism and contract vehicle used. It also includes an analysis of the industrial base for each agency, including top 10 vendor lists for each agency for 2012 (with 2011 ranks for each vendor) and analysis of cross-agency participation among the overall top 20 federal services vendors in 2002 and 2012.

Figure 4-1: Services Contracting by the Department of Defense, 2000–2012

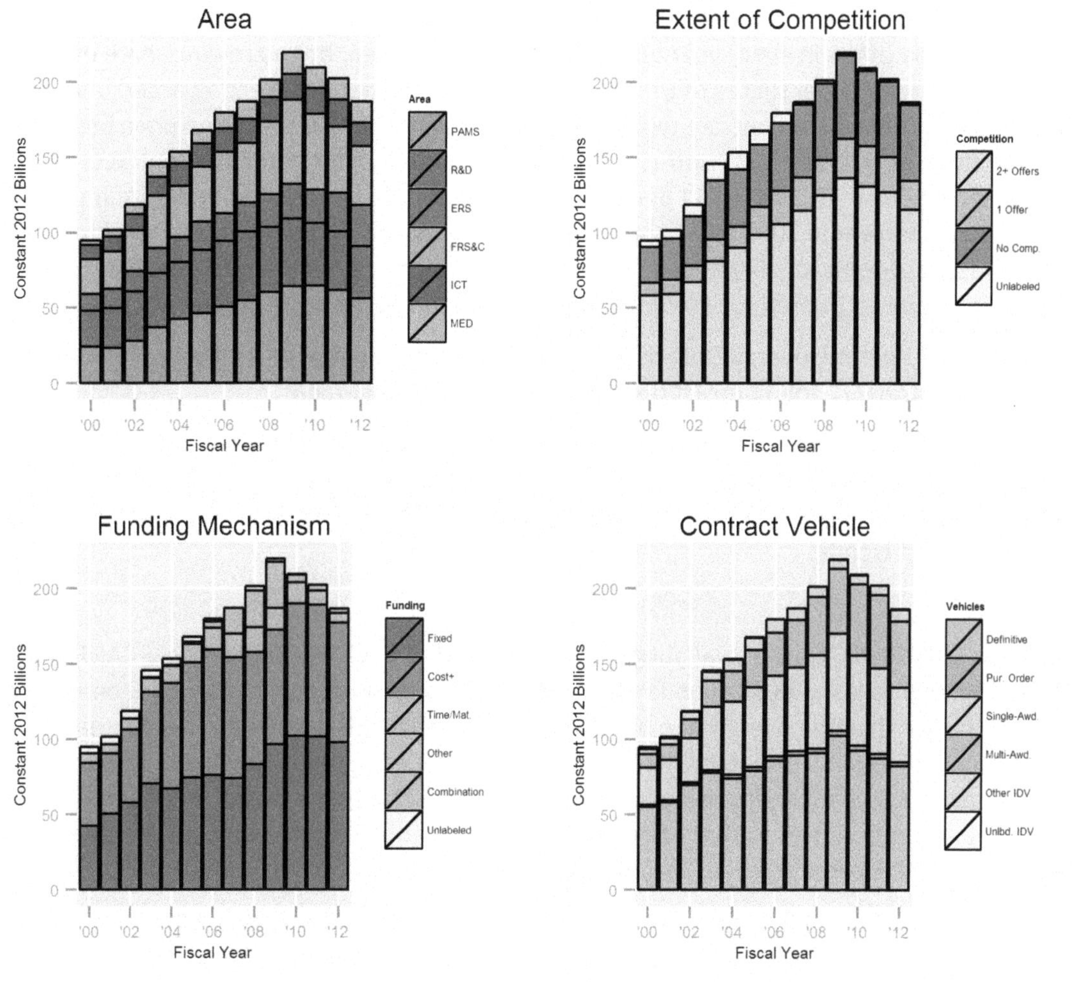

Top 10 Vendors

Vendor	2012 Millions	2011 Rank
Lockheed Martin	11,570	1
Boeing	8,350	3
Northrop Grumman	7,990	2
Raytheon	6,080	4
SAIC	4,480	5
L3 Communications	3,780	7
Humana	3,470	8
General Dynamics	3,240	6
TriWest Healthcare	3,010	9
Health Net	2,930	11
Top 10 Defense Obligations	76,110	
Total Defense Obligations	186,760	

* Joint Venture

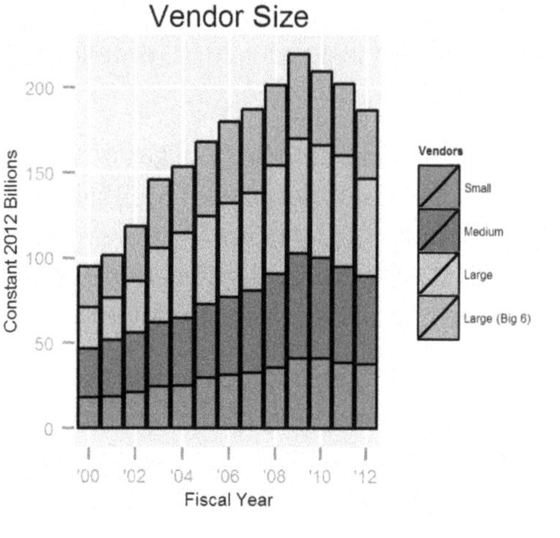

Source: FPDS; CSIS analysis.

Department of Defense

From 2000 to 2012, FFRS&C, PAMS, and R&D have each accounted for approximately a quarter of DoD services contract obligations. Over 55 percent of DoD services contract obligations were awarded after competition with multiple offers in every year during the period observed, but a growing share of that is limited competition. Roughly equal shares of DoD services contract obligations were awarded under fixed price and cost reimbursement contract types in the early and mid-2000s, but fixed price has risen steadily since. The share of DoD services contract obligations awarded under definitive contracts has fallen steadily, from 58 percent in 2000 to 44 percent in 2012, as the share awarded under multiple-award IDCs rose from 9 percent in 2000 to 24 percent in 2012. Large vendors have accounted for over 30 percent of DoD services contract obligations in most years during the period observed, while medium vendors and the Big 6 have accounted for around a quarter each throughout the period.

In the 2009–2012 period, overall DoD contract obligations declined at a -5.2 percent 3-year CAGR. Between 2011 and 2012, DoD contract obligations dropped by 8 percent.

Note that DoD services contract obligations were temporarily inflated in 2009 and 2010 due to the American Recovery and Reinvestment Act (ARRA) of 2009, which accounted for 2 percent of DoD services contract obligations in 2009 and 2010. See Chapter 5 for further discussion of the impact of ARRA on services contract trends.

Service Areas

From 2009 to 2012, DoD FRS&C contractual obligations decreased at a -11.4 percent 3-year CAGR, falling from $55.9 billion in 2009 to just $38.8 billion in 2012. DoD R&D obligations declined at a 7.9 percent 3-year CAGR, slightly higher than the overall rate of decline for DoD. DoD R&D expenditures decreased from $44.9 billion in 2009 to $35.1 billion in 2012. DoD ERS contract obligations saw the only year-on-year increase (5.8 percent 3-year CAGR), rising from $23 billion to $27.2 billion. PAMS (-4.6 percent 3-year CAGR) declined at a rate similar to that of overall DoD contract obligations, while ICT (-2.1 percent 3-year CAGR) and MED (-1.5 percent 3-year CAGR) declined more slowly.

Between 2011 and 2012, ERS (7 percent) saw the only increased contractual obligations, rising from $25.5 billion to $27.2 billion in 2012. FRS&C (-12 percent), ICT (-11 percent), R&D (-10 percent), and PAMS (-9 percent) all saw declines in obligations from the previous year, though the decline in PAMS nearly matched the overall decline in DoD contract obligations. MED (-3 percent) saw a more limited decrease between 2011 and 2012. Breaking the data down further, there were specific PSCs that saw notable declines:

- **FRS&C**—DoD FRS&C contract obligations dropped from $43.9 billion in 2011 to $38.8 billion in 2012. DoD saw major declines of $1.9 billion in "Construction of Miscellaneous Buildings" (PSC Y199/Y1JZ), and of $1.4 billion in "Construction of Other Non-Building Facilities" (PSC Y299/Y1PZ). DoD also saw significant declines in contract obligations for three additional PSCs (for building operations, electric services, and guard services) totaling over $1 billion.
- **PAMS**—DoD PAMS obligations dropped from $61.7 billion in 2011 to $55.9 billion in 2012. Within DoD, contract obligations for "System Engineering Services" (PSC R414) dropped from $3.8 billion in 2011 to $1.7 billion in 2012, a 55 percent decline. Contract obligations for "Logistics Support Services" (PSC R706) declined from $12 billion in 2011 to $9 billion in 2012, a 25 percent decline. Additionally, DoD saw significant reductions in two other PSCs (for policy review—developmental services and translation services) totaling over $900 million.
- **R&D**—DoD R&D obligations dropped from $39.2 billion in 2011 to $35.1 billion in 2012. R&D in the space sector was particularly hard hit: Space—Other (Applied Research/Exploratory

Development) (PSC AR92) dropped from $1.7 billion to $700 million, a 59 percent decline, and Space—Other (Operational Systems Development) (PSC AR95) dropped from $740 million to $270 million, a 64 percent decline. Significant decreases were also seen in three PSCs (for aircraft, electronics & communications equipment, and general engineering) totaling over $1.4 billion.

Competition

In the 2009–2012 period, contract obligations awarded after competition with multiple offers declined at a -5.2 percent 3-year CAGR, nearly matching the overall rate of decline for DoD, and accounted for 62 percent of DoD contract obligations in both 2009 and 2012. Notably, full competition with multiple offers declined sharply (-9.7 percent 3-year CAGR), while limited competition with multiple offers showed slight growth (1.2 percent 3-year CAGR). This is particularly noteworthy for DoD, where limited competition with multiple offers accounted for almost 46 percent of contract obligations awarded after competition with multiple offers. DoD services contract obligations awarded without competition declined more slowly (-2.9 percent 3-year CAGR), rising as a share of DoD contract obligations from 25 percent in 2009 to 27 percent in 2012. Contract obligations awarded after competition with a single offer declined at nearly twice the rate of overall DoD (-10.1 percent 3-year CAGR), falling as a share of DoD services contract obligations from 12 percent in 2009 to 10 percent in 2012.

Between 2011 and 2012, the share of DoD contract obligations awarded after competition with multiple offers declined from 63 percent to 62 percent, while the share awarded without competition increased from 25 percent to 27 percent. The share awarded after competition with a single offer declined from 11 percent to 10 percent.

Funding Mechanism

In the 2009–2012 period, DoD contract obligations awarded under fixed price contract types grew slightly (0.5 percent 3-year CAGR) even as overall DoD services contract obligations declined, rising as a share of overall DoD services from 44 percent in 2009 to 52 percent in 2012. Contract obligations awarded under cost reimbursement contract types grew slightly faster (1.4 percent 3-year CAGR), rising from 35 percent of DoD services contract obligations in 2009 to 43 percent in 2012. A large portion of the jump in both is attributable to the decline in combination contracts between 2009 and 2010, declining from 14 percent of contract obligations in 2009 to 2 percent or less since. Contract obligations awarded under time and materials contracts declined nearly five times as fast as overall DoD services contract obligations (-24.4 percent 3-year CAGR), dropping as a share of DoD services from 7 percent in 2009 to 3 percent in 2012.

Between 2011 and 2012, the share of DoD services contract obligations awarded under fixed price contract types rose from 50 percent to 52 percent, while cost reimbursement held steady at 43 percent. Contract obligations awarded under time and materials contracts declined from 4 percent to 3 percent.

Vehicle

In the 2009–2012 period, DoD services contract obligations awarded under definitive contracts declined slightly faster (-7.0 percent 3-year CAGR) than overall DoD services (-5.2 percent 3-year CAGR), falling as a share of overall DoD services from 47 percent in 2009 to 44 percent in 2012. Contract obligations awarded under purchase orders (-9.3 percent 3-year CAGR) and single-award IDCs (-8.6 percent 3-year CAGR) declined faster than overall DoD services, with the latter falling as a share of overall DoD services from 30 percent in 2009 to 27 percent in 2012. Contract obligations awarded under FSS and other IDVs (8.1 percent 3-year CAGR) and multiple-award IDCs (1.2 percent 3-year CAGR) increased even as overall

DoD services contract obligations decreased, with multiple-award IDCs rising as a share of overall DoD services from 19 percent in 2009 to 24 percent in 2012.

Between 2011 and 2012, the share of DoD services contract obligations awarded under definitive contracts rose from 43 percent to 44 percent, while single-award IDCs declined from 28 percent to 27 percent, and multiple-award IDCs held steady at 24 percent.

Vendor Size

In the 2009–2012 period, DoD services contract obligations awarded to large vendors declined at an equal rate to overall DoD services (-5.2 percent 3-year CAGR). Medium vendors (-5.9 percent 3-year CAGR) and the Big 6 vendors (-6.8 percent 3-year CAGR) both declined at rates only slightly faster than overall DoD services. DoD services contract obligations awarded to small vendors declined at around half the rate of overall DoD services (-2.7 percent 3-year CAGR).

Between 2011 and 2012, the share of DoD services contract obligations awarded to small vendors rose from 19 percent to 20 percent, and the share awarded to the Big 6 vendors rose from 21 percent to 22 percent. The share awarded to large vendors fell from 32 percent to 31 percent, while the share awarded to medium vendors held steady at 28 percent.

Top 10

The only change in the top 5 vendors from 2002 to 2012 is SAIC taking the place of General Dynamics. The remainder of the top 5 in 2012 shows the rise of MED contract obligations, with Humana, TriWest Healthcare, and Health Net all in the top 10 DoD vendors. The top 5 DoD services vendors accounted for 26 percent of DoD services contract obligations in 2002, but only 21 percent in 2012. Similarly, the top 10 accounted for 35 percent of overall DoD services contract obligations, but only 29 percent in 2012.

There was very little change in the top 10 DoD vendors between 2011 and 2012. Two vendors not in the top 20 in 2011 rose into the top 20 in 2012: Bechtel (23rd in 2011, 19th in 2012) and United Technologies (21st in 2011, 20th in 2012). URS saw the most significant rise, from 19th in 2011 to 15th in 2012, while ITT saw the largest decline, from 12th in 2011 to 17th in 2012, due in large part to the spinoff of their defense technology business in October 2011.

Figure 4-2: Services Contracting by the Department of Energy, 2000–2012

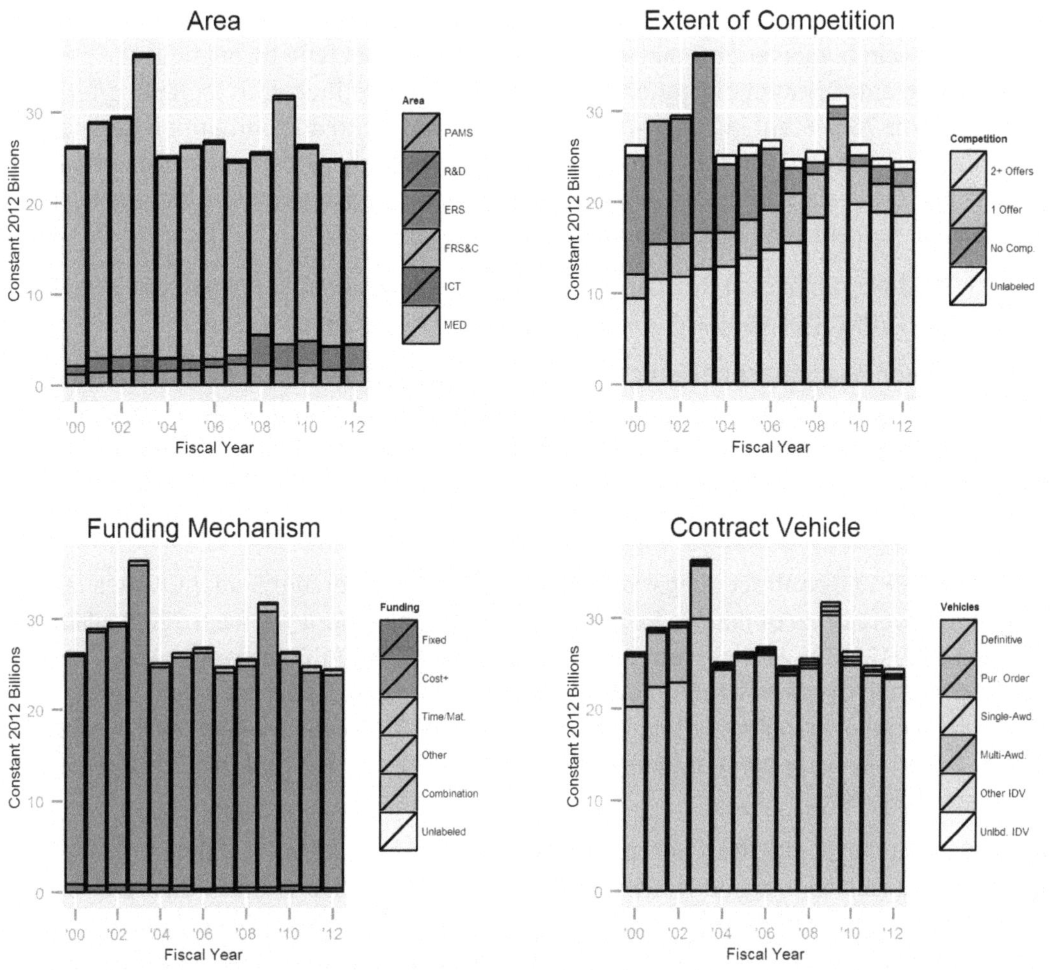

Top 10 Vendors

Vendor	2012 Millions	2011 Rank
Lockheed Martin	2,620	2
Los Alamos National Security*	2,150	1
Bechtel	1,670	3
Battelle	1,640	4
Lawrence Livermore Nat'l Sec.*	1,640	5
UT-Battelle Joint Venture*	1,250	6
URS	1,100	7
McDermott International	1,010	9
University of California	950	8
SRNS*	820	10
Top 10 Energy Obligations	20,350	
Total Energy Obligations	24,380	

* Joint Venture

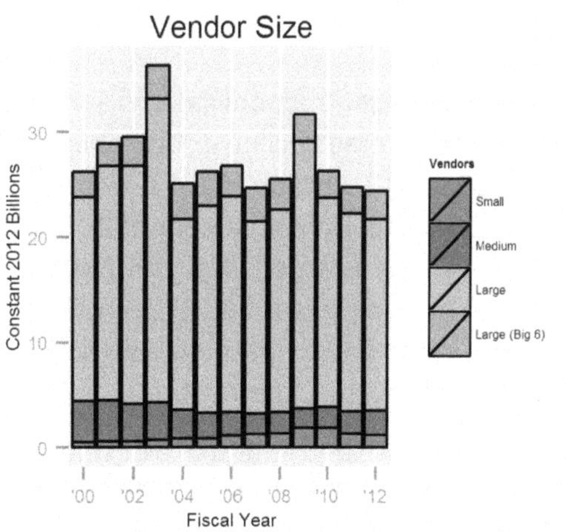

Source: FPDS; CSIS analysis.

Department of Energy

From 2000 to 2012, FRS&C accounted for an average of 86 percent of DoE services contract obligations. The share of DoE services contract obligations awarded under definitive contracts has remained steady around 97 percent. Cost reimbursement remained the dominant contract type throughout the period, remaining around 96 percent. Contract obligations awarded after competition with multiple offers rose from 36 percent in 2000 to 76 percent in 2012, while contract awards with no competition declined from 50 percent to 7 percent. Large vendors accounted for approximately 75 percent of DoE services contract obligations in most years during the period observed, while medium vendors and the Big 6 accounted for around 10 percent each throughout the period.

In the 2009–2012 period, overall DoE contract obligations declined at a -8.4 percent 3-year CAGR. Between 2011 and 2012, DoE contract obligations declined by 1.4 percent.

Note that DoE services contract obligations were temporarily inflated in 2009 and 2010 due to the American Recovery and Reinvestment Act (ARRA) of 2009, which accounted for 22 percent of DoE services contract obligations in 2009, and 4 percent in 2012. See Chapter 5 for further discussion of the impact of ARRA on services contract trends.

Service Areas

From 2009 to 2012, DoE FRS&C contract obligations decreased at a -9.7 percent 3-year CAGR, a rate slightly higher than the overall rate of decline for DoE. DoE FRS&C obligations fell from $26.9 billion in 2009 to $19.8 billion in 2012. ICT (-21.4 percent 3-year CAGR) and MED (-11.0 percent 3-year CAGR) declined at rates higher than the overall rate of decline for DoE. PAMS (-1.5 percent 3-year CAGR) declined more slowly than the overall rate of decline, while ERS (28.2 percent 3-year CAGR) and R&D (0.2 percent 3-year CAGR) saw year-on-year increases, though ERS accounted for less than 1 percent of DoE services contract obligations.

Between 2011 and 2012, ERS (40.4 percent), MED (26.2 percent), PAMS (2.7 percent), and R&D (5.7 percent) all saw increased contract obligations as DoE saw overall losses. FRS&C (-2.2 percent) declined at a rate slightly higher than the overall decline in DoE contract obligations. ICT (-43.2 percent) declined at a rate significantly higher than the overall rate of decline, though ICT represents just 1 percent of all DoE obligations.

Competition

In the 2009–2012 period, contract obligations awarded after competition with multiple offers declined at a rate even with the overall decline in DoE obligations (8.4 percent 3-year CAGR), dropping from $24.1 billion in 2009 to $18.5 billion in 2012. Contracts awarded after no competition increased at a 10.6 percent 3-year CAGR, going from 4 percent of DoE services contract obligations in 2009 to 7 percent in 2012. Contract obligations awarded after competition with a single offer (-14.2 percent 3-year CAGR) and Unlabeled (-9.9 percent 3-year CAGR) decreased at a rate higher than the overall rate of decline. Shares of DOE obligations for competition with single offer obligations decreased slightly from 16 percent of total obligations to 13 percent.

Between 2011 and 2012, the share of DoE contract obligations awarded after competition with single offer increased from 12 percent in 2011 to 13 percent in 2012. Contract obligations awarded without competition decreased from 8 percent to 7 percent, while contract obligations awarded after competition with multiple offers held steady at 76 percent.

Funding Mechanism

In the 2009–2012 period, DOE contract obligations awarded under cost reimbursement contract types decreased at a rate (-8.3 percent 3-year CAGR) similar to the overall decline in DoE. Contracts awarded under fixed price contract types (-5.3 percent 3-year CAGR) decreased more slowly than the overall, and increased from a 1 percent share of total obligations in 2009 to 2 percent in 2012. Contract obligations awarded under time and materials (-10.6 percent 3-year CAGR), combination (-21.7 percent 3-year CAGR), other (-205.0 percent 3-year CAGR), and Unlabeled (-131.5 percent 3-year CAGR) contract types all saw decreases at rates higher than the overall DoE rate of decline. The share of total obligations remained constant for all four contract types.

Between 2011 and 2012, contracts obligations awarded under cost reimbursement contract types increased as a share of overall DoE contract obligations from 95 percent to 96 percent. Time and materials contract types decreased as a share of DoE obligations from 3 percent in 2011 to 2 percent in 2012, while fixed price held steady at 2 percent.

Vehicle

In the 2009–2012 period, DoE services contract obligations awarded under definitive contracts (-8.3 percent 3-year CAGR) declined at a rate similar to the overall decline in DoE services. Contract obligations awarded under purchase orders (-21.2 percent 3-year CAGR), single-award IDCs (-12.2 percent 3-year CAGR), and multiple-award IDCs (-26.2 percent 3-year CAGR) declined at rates higher than overall rate of decline. However, contracts awarded under these three types represent a combined 2 percent of DoE services contract obligations. Contracts obligations awarded under FSS or other IDV (3.2 percent 3-year CAGR) increased as overall DoE services contract obligations decreased, but did not exceed $500 million in any year during this period.

Between 2011 and 2012, shares of DOE services contract obligations awarded under the various contract vehicle types remained constant. Contract obligations awarded under definitive contracts held steady at 96 percent, while all other contract vehicle types remained around 1 to 2 percent.

Vendor Size

In the 2009–2012 period, DoE services contract obligations awarded to medium vendors increased at a 7.5 percent 3-year CAGR, increasing as a share of DoE services contract obligations from 6 percent in 2009 to 9 percent in 2012. The Big 6 vendors saw a slight increase in obligations (0.1 percent 3-year CAGR), rising from 8 percent of DoE services contract obligations in 2009 to 11 percent in 2012. Small vendors (-13.8 percent 3-year CAGR) and large vendors (-10.3 percent 3-year CAGR) saw decreases in obligations higher than the overall rate of decline. The share of DoE services contract obligations awarded to large vendors fell from 80 percent in 2009 to 75 percent in 2012, while small vendors declined from 6 percent to 5 percent.

Between 2011 and 2012, shares of contract obligations awarded to large vendors fell from 76 percent to 75 percent, while the Big 6 vendors increased from 10 percent to 11 percent. Small and medium vendors' shares of contract obligations remained constant at 5 percent and 9 percent, respectively.

Top 10

As with FRS&C contracting, many of the top vendors for DoE in both 2002 and 2012 were involved in the management of national nuclear laboratories, although the entities managing those labs have changed. In the top 5, three companies from the top 5 in 2002 (the University of California, the Washington Savannah River Company joint venture, and the University of Chicago) were replaced in 2012 (by the Los

Alamos National Security and Lawrence Livermore National Security joint ventures, as well as Battelle). Contract obligations have been spread somewhat more widely since 2002, but are still heavily concentrated among the top vendors: the top 5 accounted for 64 percent of DoE services contract obligations in 2002, compared to 40 percent in 2012. Similarly, the top 10 vendors accounted for 80 percent of DoE services contract obligations in 2002, compared to 61 percent in 2012.

Unsurprisingly, given the types of long-term management contracts for national laboratories given out by DoE, there was little movement in the top 10 vendors between 2011 and 2012. Only one vendor moved into the top 20 from 2011 to 2012 (Stanford University—21st in 2011, 20th in 2012), and no vendor rose or fell more than three places.

Figure 4-3: Services Contracting by the Department of Health and Human Services, 2000–2012

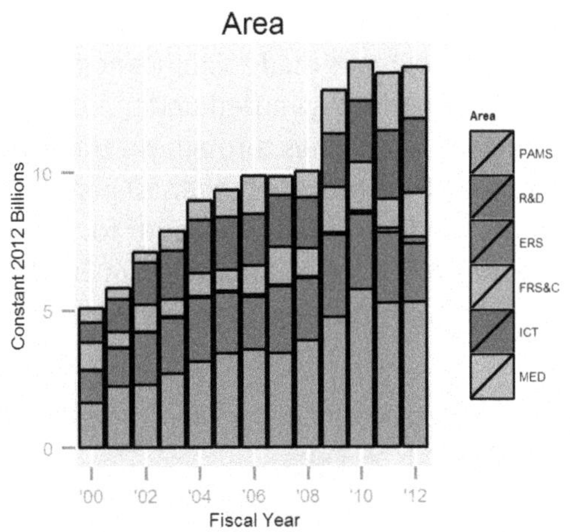

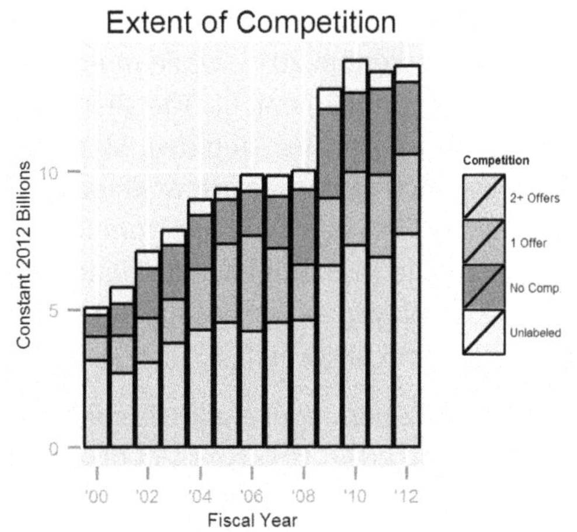

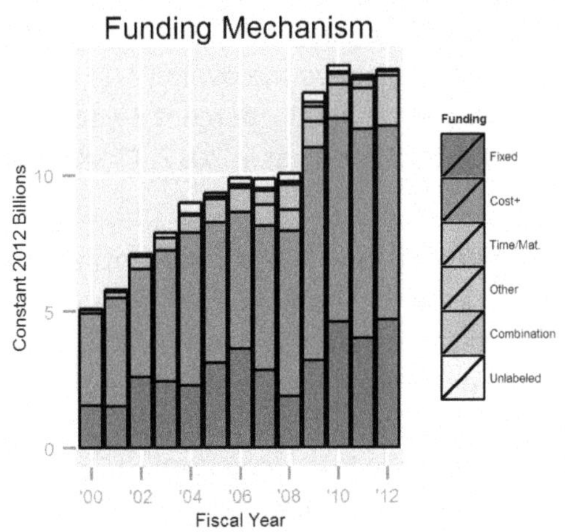

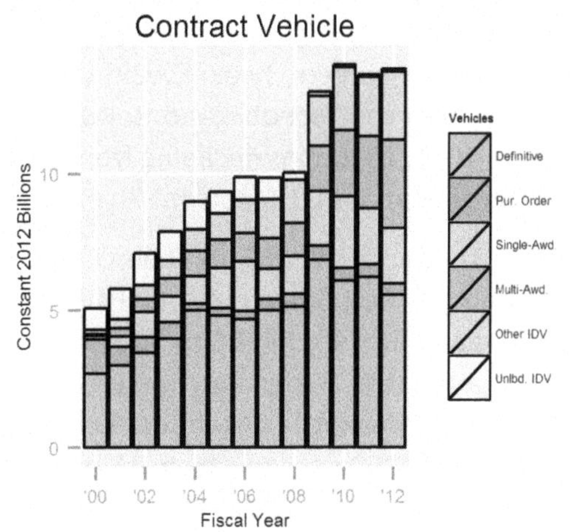

Top 10 Vendors

Vendor	2012 Millions	2011 Rank
SAIC	590	1
Lockheed Martin	310	3
RTI	270	6
Westat	260	4
Blue Cross & Blue Shield	260	5
Northrop Grumman	250	7
General Dynamics	250	>20
Emergent BioSolutions	200	--
Texas A&M	180	--
Booz Allen Hamilton	170	8
Top 10 HHS Obligations	4,120	
Total HHS Obligations	13,820	

* Joint Venture

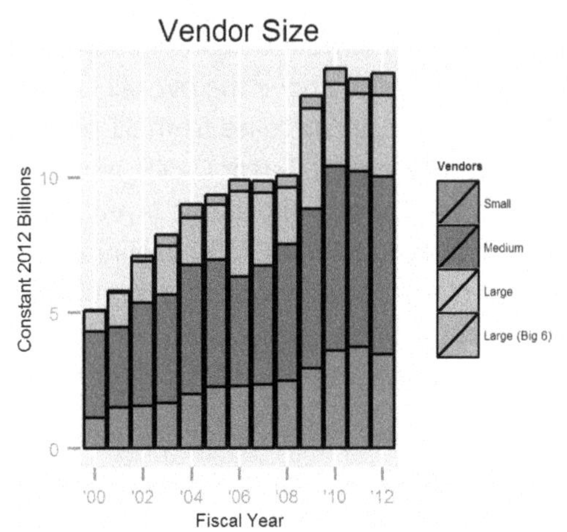

Source: FPDS; CSIS analysis.

Department of Health and Human Services

From 2000 to 2012, PAMS remained the single-largest service area for HHS, averaging around 35 percent in most years. HHS contracts awarded under definitive contracts saw decreased shares, from 53 percent in 2000 to 40 percent in 2012, while multiple-award IDC contract types made significant gains, increasing from 5 percent to 23 percent. The share of HHS contract obligations awarded under cost reimbursement contract types averaged over 50 percent, but saw gradual declines throughout the period. Contract obligations awarded after competition with multiple offers remained near 50 percent in most years, but saw declines in total share from 62 percent in 2000. Medium vendors account for the largest share of vendors in HHS, but have declined from 62 percent in 2000 to just 47 percent in 2012. The Big 6 vendors have played an increasing, but still minor, role in HHS contracting, growing from less than 1 percent in 2000 to 6 percent in 2012.

In the 2009–2012 period, overall HHS contract obligations increased at a 2.1 percent 3-year CAGR. Between 2011 and 2012, HHS contract obligations increased by 1.5 percent.

Service Area

From 2009 to 2012, HHS MED contract obligations (5.5 percent 3-year CAGR) and PAMS (3.6 percent 3-year CAGR) increased at rates slightly higher than the overall HHS rate of increase. ICT (11.9 percent 3-year CAGR) and ERS (44.4 percent 3-year CAGR) saw increases significantly above the overall rate of increase for HHS services contract obligations. R&D obligations decreased at a -10.7 percent 3-year CAGR, with the share of obligations declining from 23 percent in 2009 to 15 percent in 2012. FRS&C saw a slight decrease in obligations (-1.5 percent 3-year CAGR).

Between 2011 and 2012, ERS (62.9 percent), FRS&C (47.0 percent), and ICT (9.2 percent) all saw gains significantly above the 1.5 percent total HHS services contract growth. The share of HHS services contract obligations awarded for FRS&C increased from 8 percent to 11 percent. ICT contract obligations increased from 18 percent to 20 percent, and ERS increased from 1 percent to 2 percent. MED (-10.6 percent) and R&D (-17.0 percent) obligations declined sharply, with the share of HHS contract obligations awarded for MED declining from 15 percent to 13 percent, while R&D decreased to 15 percent from 19 percent in 2012. PAMS saw a slight increase (0.5 percent) from the previous year.

Competition

In the 2009–2012 period, contract obligations awarded after competition with multiple offers increased at a 5.4 percent 3-year CAGR, above the overall rate of increase for HHS, and accounted for 56 percent of HHS obligations in 2012, an increase from 51 percent in 2009. Notably, full competition with multiple offers declined at a -0.4 percent 3-year CAGR, while contracts awarded under limited competition with multiple offers increased at a 15.6 percent 3-year CAGR. Contracts awarded without competition decreased at a -6.8 percent 3-year CAGR, declining as a share of HHS services contract obligations from 25 percent to 19 percent. The share of contract obligations awarded after competition with a single offer increased moderately (6.3 percent 3-year CAGR), rising as a share of overall HHS services contract obligations from 19 percent in 2009 to 21 percent in 2012.

Between 2011 and 2012, HHS services contract obligations awarded after competition with multiple offers increased from 51 percent in 2011 to 56 percent in 2012. Contract obligations awarded after no competition decreased from 23 percent to 19 percent in 2012. Contract obligations awarded after competition with single offer and unlabeled awards declined from 22 percent to 21 percent and from 5 percent to 4 percent, respectively.

Funding Mechanism

In the 2009–2012 period, HHS contract obligations awarded under fixed price contract types grew at a 13.5 percent 3-year CAGR, significantly higher than the overall HHS increase. The share of HHS services contract obligations for fixed price contracts grew from 25 percent in 2009 to 34 percent in 2012. Contract obligations awarded under cost reimbursement contract types decreased at a -3.1 percent 3-year CAGR, declining as a share of HHS obligations from 60 percent in 2009 to 51 percent in 2012. Contract obligations awarded under time and materials contracts grew significantly (24.6 percent 3-year CAGR), increasing as a share of HHS services contract obligations from 7 percent to 13 percent. Other (-32.1 percent 3-year CAGR), combination (-43.8 percent 3-year CAGR), and unlabeled (-64.9 percent 3-year CAGR) all saw significant declines in over the period.

Between 2011 and 2012, the share of HHS contract obligations awarded under fixed price contract types increased to 34 percent in 2012 from 29 percent in 2011. Contracts awarded under cost reimbursement decreased from 56 percent to 51 percent, while the share of contract obligations awarded under time and materials contracts increased from 11 percent to 13 percent.

Vehicle

In the 2009–2012 period, HHS services contract obligations awarded under definitive contracts declined (-6.7 percent 3-year CAGR) as overall HHS services contract obligations rose. Definitive contracts fell as a share of HHS services contract obligations from 53 percent in 2009 to 40 percent in 2012. Contract obligations awarded under multiple-award IDCs grew at a rate much higher (24.9 percent 3-year CAGR) than overall HHS services, rising as a share of HHS services contract obligations from 13 percent in 2009 to 23 percent in 2012. Contract obligations awarded under purchase orders (-5.1 percent 3-year CAGR) and unlabeled IDVs (-12.6 percent 3-year CAGRs) saw decreases, while FSS or other IDVs (11.0 percent 3-year CAGRs) and single-award IDCs (0.2 percent 3-year CAGR) saw increases.

Between 2011 and 2012, the share of contract obligations awarded under multiple-award IDCs increased from 19 percent to 23 percent, while definitive contracts fell from 46 percent to 40 percent. Contracts awarded under FSS or other IDV contract types increased slightly, from 16 percent to 18 percent, while purchase orders, single-award IDCs, and unlabeled IDVs remained constant at 3 percent, 15 percent, and 1 percent, respectively.

Vendor Size

In the 2009–2012 period, only large vendors (-7.0 percent 3-year CAGR) saw decreases in obligations, falling as a share of HHS services contract obligations from 29 percent in 2009 to 22 percent in 2012. Medium vendors continued to remain the largest share of HHS obligations, growing slightly (3.8 percent 3-year CAGR) and rising as share of overall HHS services contract obligations from 45 percent in 2009 to 47 percent in 2012. Contract obligations awarded to the Big 6 vendors grew strongly (19.1 percent 3-year CAGR), while small vendors saw moderate growth (5.6 percent 3-year CAGR).

Between 2011 and 2012, the share of HHS service contract obligations awarded to the Big 6 vendors increased from 4 percent to 6 percent. Meanwhile, the share awarded to small firms decreased from 28 percent in 2011 to 25 percent in 2012. The shares awarded to large firms slightly increased from 21 percent to 22 percent, while medium firms remained constant at 47 percent of HHS service contract obligations.

Top 10

There was moderate turnover in the top 5 vendors between 2002 and 2012, with two top 5 vendors from 2002 (Acambis and Gilbane Building Company) replaced (by Lockheed Martin and Blue Cross &

Blue Shield). Northrop Grumman was the only vendor in the rest of the top 10 in 2002 to remain there in 2012. The share of HHS contract obligations awarded to the top 5 has declined, from 20 percent in 2002 to 12 percent in 2012, as has the share awarded to the top 10, from 27 percent in 2002 to 20 percent in 2012.

The top 5 in 2012 saw mostly minor shifts from 2011, with RTI rising to 3rd (from 6th in 2011). Vangent, which ranked 2nd in 2011, fell to 18th in 2012 after it was purchased by General Dynamics (48th in 2011, 7th in 2012) in August 2011. Five other vendors not among the top 20 HHS vendors in 2011 rose into the top 20 in 2012: Emergent Biosolutions (outside the top 100 in 2011, 8th in 2012), Texas A&M (outside the top 100 in 2011, 9th in 2012), Noridian (outside the top 100 in 2011, 14th in 2012), GHI Medicare (29th in 2011, 16th in 2012), and Celerian Group (27th in 2011, 20th in 2012). Other significant changes occurred for Highmark (18th in 2011, 11th in 2012) and HP (12th in 2011, 19th in 2012).

Figure 4-4: Services Contracting by the Department of Homeland Security, 2000–2012

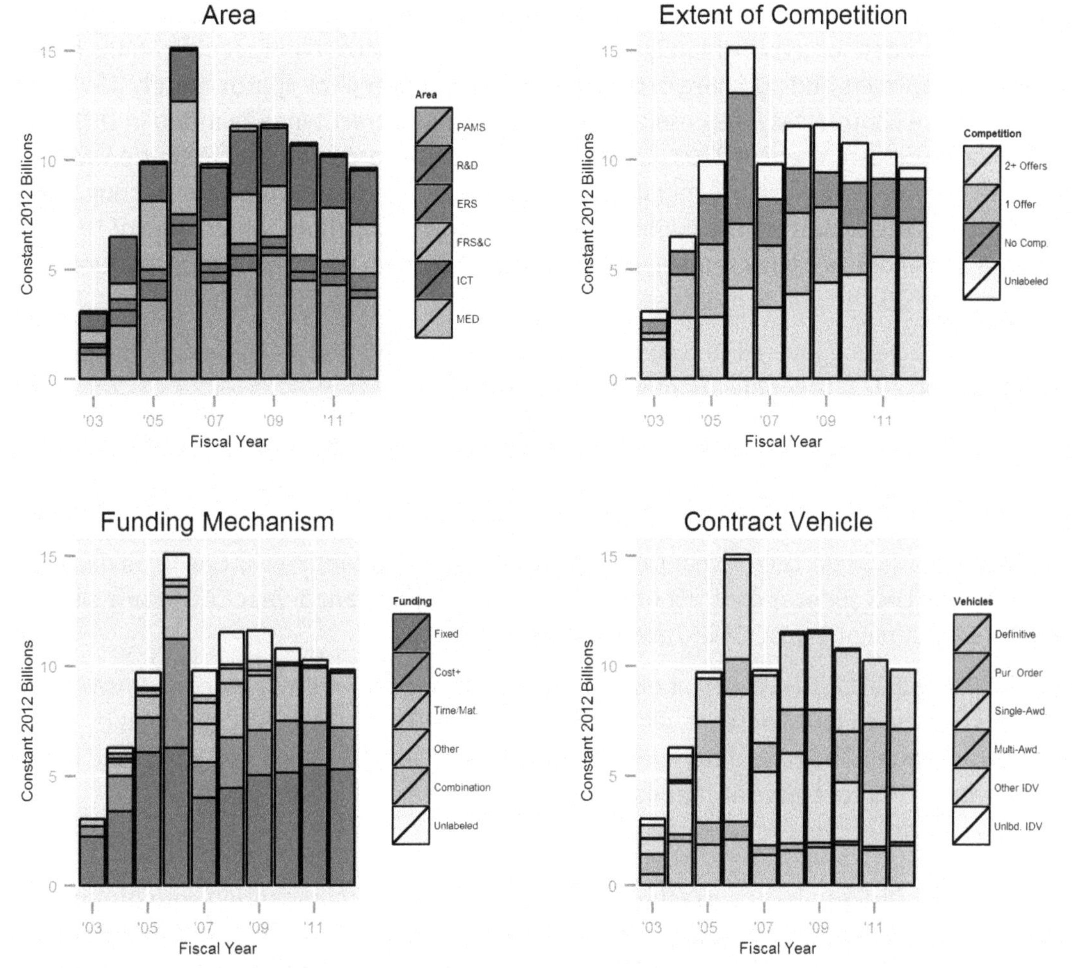

Top 10 Vendors

Vendor	2012 Millions	2011 Rank
Computer Sciences Corp.	670	1
Lockheed Martin	400	3
SAIC	280	4
IBM	280	2
Securitas AB	210	6
General Dynamics	190	7
Hewlett-Packard	190	5
GEO Group	180	9
Booz Allen Hamilton	160	8
Unisys	140	12
Top 10 DHS Obligations	3,780	
Total DHS Obligations	9,640	

* Joint Venture

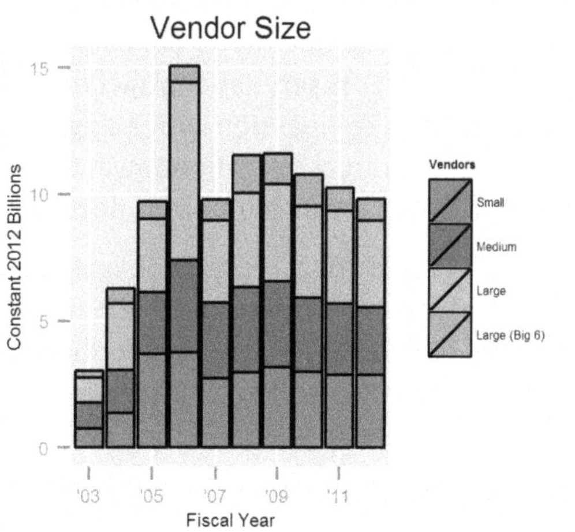

Source: FPDS; CSIS analysis.

Department of Homeland Security

From 2003 to 2012, PAMS accounted for nearly 40 percent of DHS service contract obligations in most years, with FRS&C and ICT each accounting for approximately 25 percent. Contracts awarded under multiple-award IDC accounted for approximately 40 percent of DHS services contract obligations in most years, while definitive contracts and purchase orders have each accounted for approximately 25 percent. While fixed price contracts still represent 54 percent of all contract types awarded in DHS, they have declined from a 73 percent share in 2003. Contract obligations awarded after competition with multiple offers have declined sharply in the middle of the decade due to post-Katrina contracting, but has gradually rebounded to account for the majority of DHS contract obligations. The shares of DHS contract obligations by vendor size have remained relatively steady, with large vendors accounting for the largest share, around 35 percent, in most years.

In the 2009–2012 period, overall DHS contract obligations declined at a -5.4 percent 3-year CAGR. Between 2011 and 2012, DHS obligations fell by 6 percent.

Service Areas

From 2009 to 2012, DHS PAMS contract obligations decreased at a -13.3 percent 3-year CAGR, falling as a share of DHS services contract obligations from 49 percent in 2009 to 38 percent in 2012. FRS&C (-0.9 percent 3-year CAGR), ICT (-2.8 percent 3-year CAGR), and MED (-0.8 percent 3-year CAGR) all declined more slowly than overall DHS services contract obligations. R&D (1.2 percent 3-year CAGR) saw slight growth, while ERS (14.9 percent 3-year CAGR) grew strongly.

Between 2011 and 2012, DHS contract obligations for ERS increased by 24 percent. PAMS contract obligations decreased by 14 percent, while R&D declined 29 percent. FRS&C declined by 7 percent, similar to the overall DHS rate of decline. MED (3 percent) and ICT (5 percent) increased in obligations while overall DHS contract obligations declined.

Competition

In the 2009–2012 period, DHS services contract obligations awarded after competition with multiple offers increased at an 8.0 percent 3-year CAGR, rising as a share of DHS services contract obligations from 38 percent in 2009 to 57 percent in 2012. DHS contract obligations awarded without competition (7.8 percent 3-year CAGR) grew at a similar rate, while competition with single offer (-22.3 percent 3-year CAGR) and unlabeled competition (-38.4 percent 3-year CAGR) saw declines significantly above the overall rate of decline for DHS services contract obligations. The share of DHS services contract obligations awarded after competition with a single offer decreased from 30 percent in 2009 to 17 percent in 2012, while contract obligations awarded without competition grew from 14 percent in 2009 to 20 percent in 2012, and unlabeled awards decreased from 19 percent in 2009 from 5 percent in 2012.

Between 2011 and 2012, contract obligations awarded after competition with multiple offers increased from 54 percent to 57 percent of DHS obligations. Meanwhile, unlabeled contract obligations declined from 11 percent to 5 percent. Competition with a single offer held steady at 17 percent, while contract obligations awarded without competition rose from 17 percent to 20 percent.

Funding Mechanism

In the 2009–2012 period, DHS services contract obligations awarded under fixed price contract types grew at a 1.8 percent 3-year CAGR while overall DHS services contract obligations decreased, increasing as a share from 43 percent to 54 percent. Contract obligations awarded under cost reimbursement contract types (-2.8 percent 3-year CAGR) declined more slowly than DHS services contract obligations overall, while time and materials held steady (0.0 percent 3-year CAGR). Combination contract, which accounted for 3 percent of DHS services contract obligations in 2009, accounted for less than 1 percent in 2012.

Between 2011 and 2012, the share of DHS services contract obligations awarded under time and materials rose from 24 percent to 26 percent. Fixed price rose from 53 percent to 54 percent, while cost reimbursement held steady at 19 percent.

Vehicle

In the 2009–2012 period, DHS services contract obligations awarded under multiple-award IDCs declined at a rate significantly faster (-13.3 percent 3-year CAGR) than the overall rate of DHS decline. The share of DHS services contract obligations awarded under multiple-award IDCs declined from a peak of 49 percent in 2009 to 38 percent in 2012. Contract obligations awarded under definitive contracts increased at a 2.3 percent 3-year CAGR, as the share of contract obligations awarded under definitive contracts increased from 24 percent in 2009 to 31 percent in 2012. FSS and other IDVs increased at a 1.2 percent 3-year CAGR, while purchase orders declined at a -2.8 percent 3-year CAGR, slower than the overall rate of decline for DHS services contract obligations. Single-award IDCs, which declined slightly (-0.8 percent 3-year CAGR), did not account for more than 1 percent of DHS services contract obligations during this period.

Between 2011 and 2012, the share of DHS services contract obligations awarded under multiple-award IDCs fell from 42 percent to 38 percent, while definitive contracts increased from 29 percent to 31 percent. The share of DHS services contract obligations awarded under purchase orders increased from 23 percent to 25 percent, while FSS or other IDVs declined from 5 percent to 4 percent.

Vendors Size

In the 2009–2012 period, DHS contract obligations awarded to medium vendors (-7.8 percent 3-year CAGR) and the Big 6 vendors (-11.2 percent 3-year CAGR) declined at rates higher than the overall rate of decline for DHS services contract obligations. Small vendors (-3.1 percent 3-year CAGR) and large vendors (-3.1 percent 3-year CAGR) declined at rates slower than the overall rate of decline for DHS services contract obligations.

Between 2011 and 2012, the share of DHS services contract obligations awarded to small vendors increased from 28 percent to 29 percent, while medium vendors declined from 28 percent to 27 percent. Large vendors declined from 36 percent to 35 percent, while the Big 6 vendors held steady at 9 percent.

Top 10

Of the top 5 vendors for DHS in 2005, only IBM remains in the top 10 in 2012, with Circle B, Unisys, Clearbook, and the Integrated Coast Guard Systems joint venture dropping out, replaced by Computer Sciences Corp., Lockheed Martin, SAIC, and Securitas AB. As a share of overall DHS services contract obligations, the top 5 accounted for 24 percent in 2005, but only 19 percent in 2012, while the top 10 declined from 35 percent in 2005 to 29 percent in 2012.

The top 5 DHS services vendors saw only slight turnover between 2011 and 2012, with Securitas AB (6th in 2011, 5th in 2012) replacing HP (5th in 2011, 7th in 2012). Three companies that were not among the top 20 DHS services vendors in 2011 rose into the top 20 in 2012: L3 Communications (22nd in 2011, 13th in 2012), Chenga (outside the top 100 in 2011, 14th in 2012), and MVM (24th in 2011, 20th in 2012). The largest decline was seen for Defense Support Services, which fell from 11th in 2011 to 18th in 2012.

Figure 4-5: Services Contracting by the General Services Administration, 2000–2012

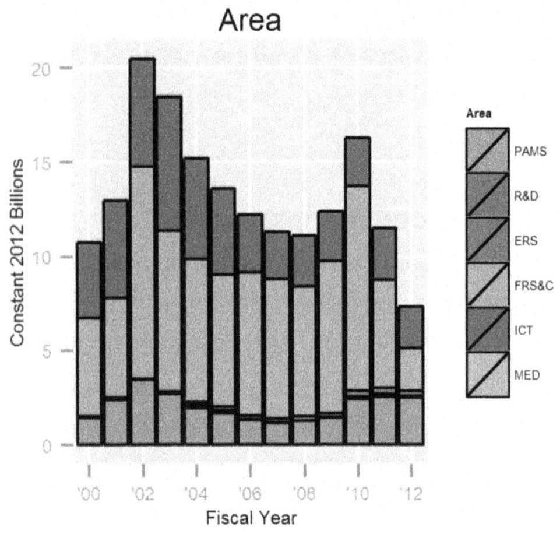

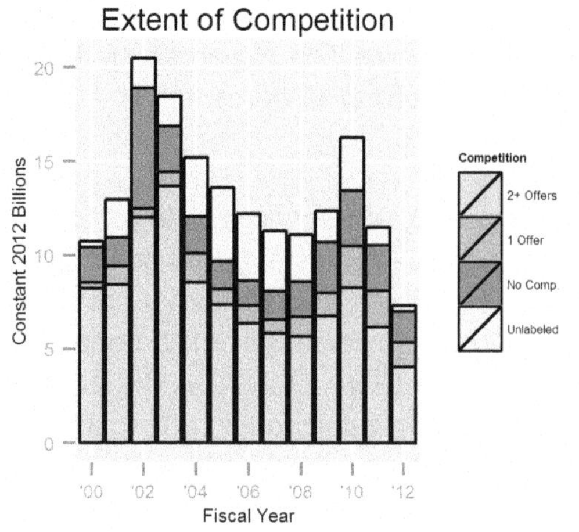

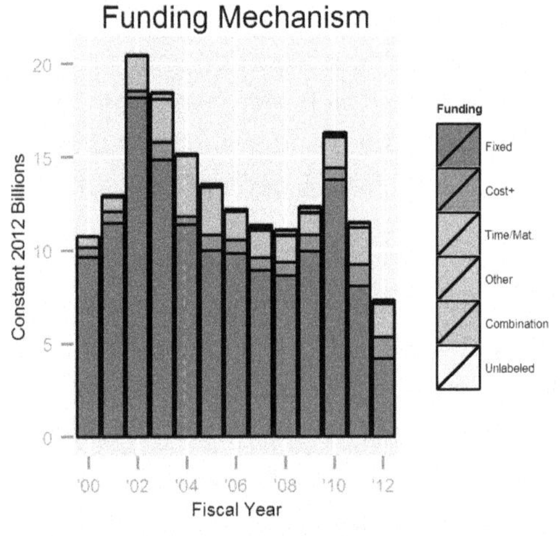

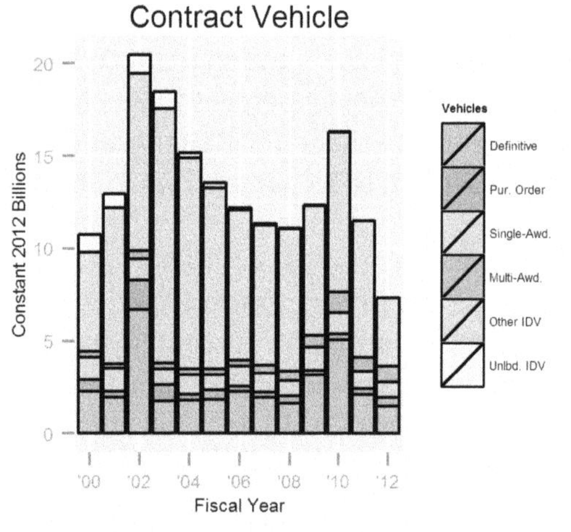

Top 10 Vendors

Vendor	2012 Millions	2011 Rank
SAIC	600	1
Hensel Phelps	360	3
Booz Allen Hamilton	300	7
SRA International	300	8
Lockheed Martin	230	4
Northrop Grumman	230	5
General Dynamics	210	2
Hewlett-Packard	180	6
ARINC	170	9
CACI	130	15
Top 10 GSA Obligations	3,410	
Total GSA Obligations	7,350	

* Joint Venture

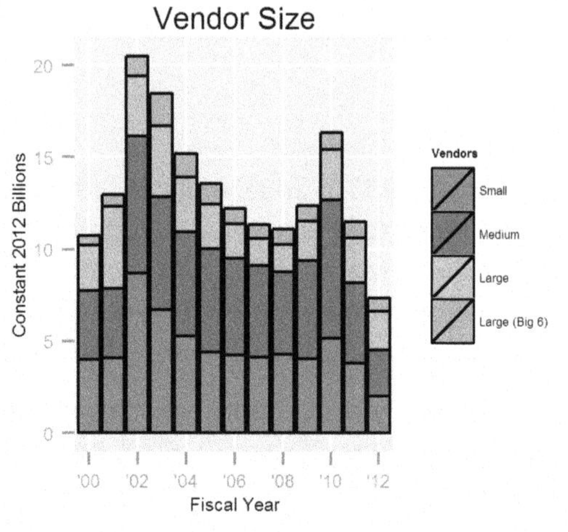

Source: FPDS; CSIS analysis.

General Services Administration

From 2000 to 2012, over half of GSA contract obligations in most years have been awarded for FRS&C, with a significant but declining share awarded for ICT. Over half of GSA contract obligations have been awarded after competition with multiple offers throughout the period. Over 75 percent of GSA contract obligations were awarded under fixed price contract types in every year but one until 2011. Over half, and as much as three quarters of GSA contract obligations have been awarded under FSS or other IDVs in all but one year. Medium vendors have accounted for a the largest share of GSA contract obligations through most of the period observed, and small vendors have accounted for nearly a third of contract obligations in most years.

GSA experienced a notable decline between 2011 and 2012 that merits further discussion. GSA services contract obligations declined from $11.5 billion in 2011 to $7.3 billion in 2012, a 36 percent decrease, almost entirely in FRS&C.[6] The primary driver of this decline is a near disappearance of obligations for "Lease of Office Buildings" (PSC X111/X1AA), which dropped from $4.7 billion in 2010 to $3.2 billion in 2011 to $13 million in 2012. This is apparently the result of a decision by GSA to stop reporting leases of office buildings into FPDS; in conversations with GSA, officials cited FAR 4.606(b)(3), which states that "lease and supplemental lease agreements for real property" may be submitted to FPDS, but submission is not required. **Though GSA finds legitimate legal justification in FAR 4.606(b)(3) to stop reporting contracts for lease of office buildings into FPDS, this represents a large step backwards for data transparency. The FY 2010 obligations total for lease of office building, if added to FY 2012 totals, would represent 39 percent of GSA's total services contract obligations, and 67 percent of GSA's FRS&C contract obligations. It would also represent 1.5 percent of total federal services contract obligations.**

The removal from of FPDS of $4.7 billion in GSA contract obligations severely distorts the following analysis of GSA contracting trends from 2009 to 2012. Given the lack of visibility available into the characteristics of the GSA contract obligations removed from FPDS, **this section will analyze the data on GSA services contract obligations that is available through FPDS, with the caveat that it does not represent a complete picture of GSA services contracting.**

In the 2009–2012 period, GSA services contract obligations declined sharply (-15.9 percent 3-year CAGR). Between 2011 and 2012, contract obligations declined by 36 percent.

Note that GSA services contract obligations were temporarily inflated in 2009 and 2010 due to the American Recovery and Reinvestment Act (ARRA) of 2009, which accounted for 13 percent of GSA services contract obligations in 2009 and 24 percent in 2010. See Chapter 5 for further discussion of the impact of ARRA on services contract trends.

Service Areas

In the 2009–2012 period, GSA services contract obligations for FRS&C declined sharply (-34.4 percent 3-year CAGR), though this is distorted by the removal of office leases from FPDS by GSA, as detailed above. GSA ICT contract obligations also declined (-5.2 percent 3-year CAGR), while contract obligations for PAMS increased significantly (21.2 percent 3-year CAGR). ERS, R&D, and MED all saw increases in the period, but none of the three exceeded $300 million in any given year.

---

[6] GSA contract obligations in 2009 and 2010 were notably inflated by funds from the American Recovery and Reinvestment Act of 2009, which boosted GSA contract obligations for construction and maintenance/repair/alteration of office buildings by $1.2 billion in 2009 and $3.1 billion in 2010.

Between 2011 and 2012, GSA FRS&C contract obligations declined by 60 percent, largely due to the issues discussed above. PAMS contract obligations were nearly stagnant (-1 percent), while ICT contract obligations declined sharply (-20 percent).

Competition

In the 2009–2012 period, both GSA contract obligations awarded after competition with multiple offers (-15.9 percent 3-year CAGR) and without competition (-14.9 percent) declined at rates similar to that of overall GSA services contract obligations. Interestingly, a large share of the GSA contract obligations removed from FPDS appear to have been awarded after full competition with multiple offers, such that competition with limited offers accounted for 72 percent of total contract obligations awarded after competition with multiple offers in 2012, compared to 47 percent in 2011. GSA services contract obligations awarded after competition with a single offer have increased slightly (2.3 percent 3-year CAGR), rising as a share of overall GSA services contract obligations from 10 percent in 2009 to 18 percent in 2012.

Between 2011 and 2012, the share of contract obligations awarded after competition with multiple offers rose from 54 percent to 55 percent, while contract obligations awarded without competition rose from 21 percent to 22 percent.

Funding Mechanism

In the 2009–2012 period, GSA services contract obligations awarded under fixed price contract types declined sharply (-24.9 percent 3-year CAGR), though it appears the removal of GSA office building leases from FPDS is a large factor in the decline. Contract obligations awarded under both cost reimbursement contract types (8.5 percent 3-year CAGR) and time and materials contracts (15.9 percent 3-year CAGR) grew strongly.

Between 2011 and 2012, the share of GSA services contract obligations awarded under fixed price contract types declined from 70 percent to 57 percent. The share awarded under cost reimbursement contract types rose from 10 percent to 15 percent, and the share awarded under time and materials contracts rose from 18 percent to 25 percent.

Vehicle

In the 2009–2012 period, GSA services contract obligations awarded under definitive contracts (-22.6 percent 3-year CAGR) and FSS and other IDVs (-19.4 percent 3-year CAGR) declined faster than overall GSA services contract obligations, with FSS and other IDVs heavily influenced by the removal of GSA office building leases from FPDS. Single-award IDCs (-13.4 percent 3-year CAGR) declined slightly more slowly than overall GSA, while purchase orders (25.4 percent 3-year CAGR) and multiple-award IDCs (13.2 percent 3-year CAGR) grew strongly.

Between 2011 and 2012, the share of GSA services contract obligations awarded under definitive contracts rose from 18 percent to 20 percent. Increases in share also occurred for purchase orders (3 percent to 6 percent), single-award IDCs (8 percent to 11 percent), and multiple-award IDCs (6 percent to 12 percent). The share of contract obligations awarded under FSS and other IDVs dropped from 64 percent to 50 percent.

Vendor Size

In the 2009–2012 period, GSA services contract obligations awarded to both small vendors (-20.7 percent 3-year CAGR) and medium vendors (-22.1 percent 3-year CAGR) saw significant declines, in large part due to the removal of GSA office building leases from FPDS. The Big 6 vendors (-4.6 percent 3-year CAGR) and large vendors (-1.1 percent 3-year CAGR) saw significantly smaller declines.

Between 2011 and 2012, the share of GSA services contract obligations awarded to small vendors declined from 33 percent to 27 percent, while the share awarded to medium vendors declined from 38 percent to 34 percent. The share awarded to large vendors rose from 21 percent to 28 percent, while the share awarded to the Big 6 vendors rose from 8 percent to 10 percent.

Top 10

There was significant turnover in the top 5 vendors for GSA between 2002 and 2012. The Association for Service Disabled Veterans, Acepex Management, and Computer Sciences Corp. fell out of the top 5 (and the top 20 entirely), replaced by Hensel Phelps, Booz Allen Hamilton, and SRA International. This trend extends to the rest of the top 10, where four of the next five vendors from 2002 (Cetrom, Quantum Research International, Dick Enterprises, and Dyncorp International) are not even in the top 20 in 2012. As a share of overall GSA services contract obligations, the share going to the top 5 vendors declined from 31 percent in 2002 to 24 percent in 2012. Similarly, the share going to the top 10 declined from 41 percent to 37 percent.

Two companies rose into the top 5 between 2011 and 2012: Booz Allen Hamilton (7th in 2011, 3rd in 2012 and SRA International (8th in 2011, 4th in 2012), replacing Northrop Grumman (5th in 2011, 6th in 2012) and General Dynamics (2nd in 2011, 7th in 2012). There were three companies outside the top 20 in 2011 who rose into the top 20 in 2012: Systems Group (outside the top 100 in 2011, 16th in 2012), Jacobs Engineering Group (24th in 2011, 18th in 2012), and Deloitte (29th in 2011, 19th in 2012).

Figure 4-6: Services Contracting by the Department of State and USAID, 2000–2012

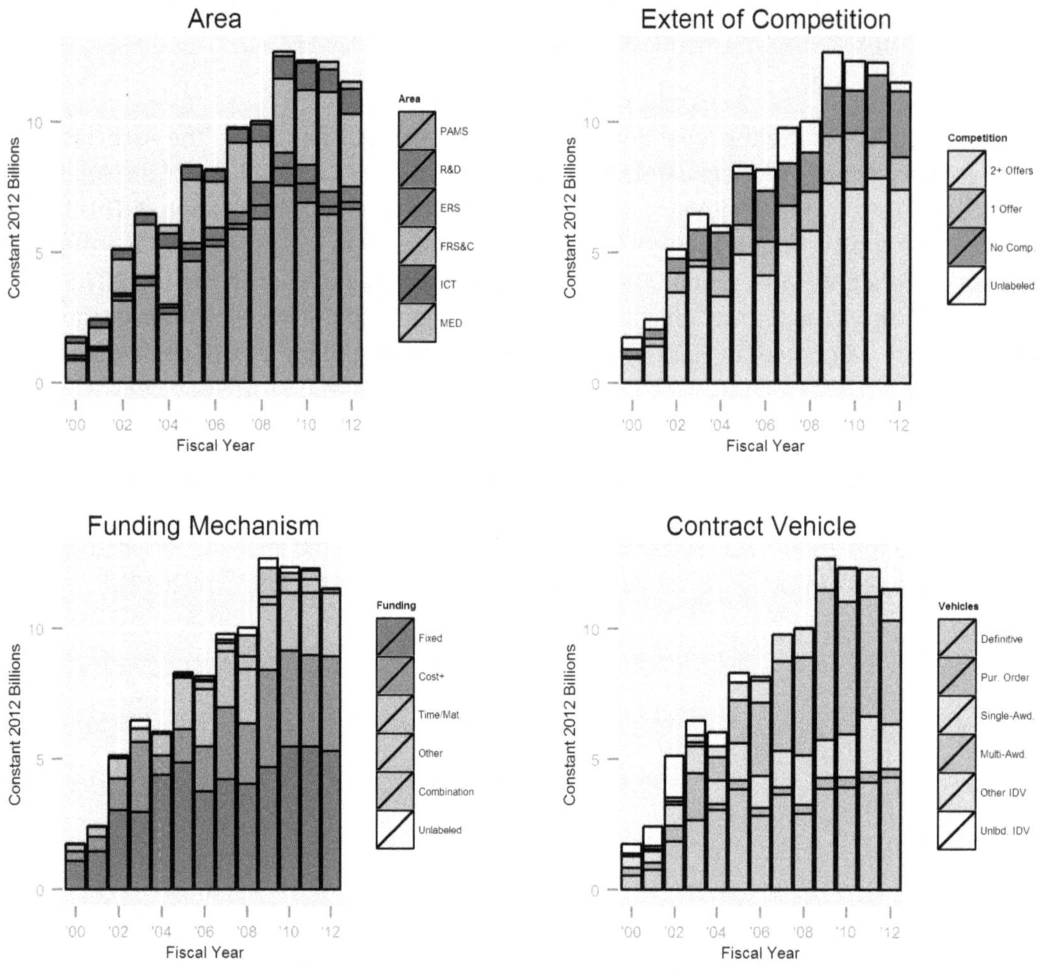

Top 10 Vendors

Vendor	2012 Millions	2011 Rank
Chemonics International	660	3
Dyncorp International	650	1
BL Harbert International	630	2
PFSCM*	430	6
Lockheed Martin	370	4
Development Alternatives Group	250	7
SAIC	250	>20
John Snow	240	10
AICI-SP	220	--
Triple Canopy	220	5
Top 10 State&USAID Obligations	5,640	
Total State&USAID Obligations	11,540	

* Joint Venture

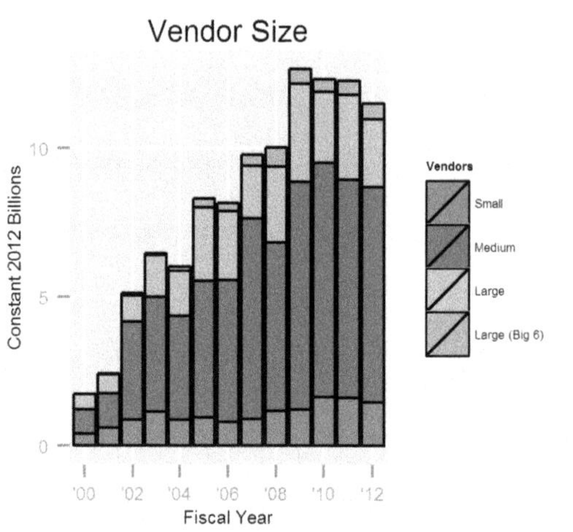

Source: FPDS; CSIS analysis.

Department of State/USAID

In the 2000–2012 period, over half of State/USAID services contract obligations were awarded for PAMS in most years. Over 55 percent of State/USAID services contract obligations were awarded after competition with multiple offers in most years during this period. Over 40 percent of State/USAID services contract obligations have been awarded under fixed price contract types in most years, but that share has varied significantly, rising as high as 73 percent in 2004, but not exceeding 46 percent since 2005. The use of multiple-award IDCs has risen rapidly throughout the period, from only 1 percent in 2000 to a high of 45 percent in 2009, though use has declined in the last three years. Since 2002, over 55 percent of State/USAID services contract obligations have been awarded to medium vendors.

In the 2009–2012 period, State/USAID services contract obligations declined at a -3.1 percent 3-year CAGR. Between 2011 and 2012, State/USAID services contract obligations declined by 6 percent, from $12.3 billion to $11.5 billion.

Service Areas

In the 2009–2012 period, State/USAID services contract obligations for PAMS declined at a rate similar to that of overall State/USAID services contract obligations (-4.2 percent 3-year CAGR). R&D declined steeply (-26.8 percent 3-year CAGR), while FRS&C declined more slowly than overall State/USAID services contract obligations (-0.7 percent 3-year CAGR). State/USAID services contract obligations awarded for ERS (1.0 percent 3-year CAGR) and ICT (4.3 percent 3-year CAGR) grew slightly, while MED (17.8 percent 3-year CAGR) grew strongly, though MED contract obligations never exceeded $300 million.

Between 2011 and 2012, State/USAID services contract obligations awarded for FRS&C (-27 percent) and R&D (-16 percent) declined sharply. MED (-7 percent) declined at a rate comparable to that of overall State/USAID services contract obligations. PAMS (3 percent), ERS (7 percent), and ICT (11 percent) all saw growth, even as overall State/USAID services contract obligations declined.

Competition

In the 2009–2012 period, State/USAID services contract obligations awarded after competition with multiple offers declined slightly (-1.0 percent 3-year CAGR), albeit more slowly than overall State/USAID services contract obligations, rising as a share of overall State/USAID services contract obligations from 60 percent in 2009 to 64 percent in 2012. Unlike for most other government agencies and service areas, full competition with multiple offers (0.9 percent 3-year CAGR) showed growth, whereas limited competition with multiple offers (-3.2 percent 3-year CAGR) declined. State/USAID services contract obligations awarded without competition grew strongly (10.8 percent 3-year CAGR), growing as a share of overall State/USAID services contract obligations from 15 percent in 2009 to 22 percent in 2012, largely due to better data labeling. State/USAID services contract obligations awarded after competition with a single offer declined sharply (-11.6 percent 3-year CAGR), while unlabeled contracts, which accounted for 11 percent of State/USAID services contract obligations in 2009, declined to 3 percent by 2012.

Between 2011 and 2012, the shares of State/USAID services contract obligations awarded after competition with multiple offers and with a single offer held steady at 64 percent and 11 percent, respectively. The share awarded without competition rose from 21 percent to 22 percent.

Funding Mechanism

In the 2009–2012 period, State/USAID services contract obligations awarded under fixed price contract types grew at a 4.1 percent 3-year CAGR, rising as a share of overall State/USAID services contract obligations from 37 percent in 2009 to 46 percent in 2012, largely due to better data labeling. State/USAID services contract obligations awarded under cost reimbursement contract types declined more slowly than overall State/USAID services contract obligations (-0.9 percent 3-year CAGR), as did time and materials (-0.6 percent 3-year CAGR). Combination contracts, which accounted for 9 percent of State/USAID services contract obligations in 2009, fell to 1 percent by 2012.

Between 2011 and 2012, the shares of State/USAID services contract obligations awarded under fixed price contract types (44 percent to 46 percent), cost reimbursement contract types (29 percent to 31 percent), and time and materials contracts (19 percent to 21 percent) all increased. These increases were largely driven by reductions in combination/other/unlabeled labeling, meaning that the increases are in large part due to better data quality rather than any specific trend.

Vehicle

In the 2009–2012 period, State/USAID services contract obligations awarded under purchase orders (-6.5 percent 3-year CAGR) and multiple-award IDCs (-11.6 percent 3-year CAGR) declined faster than overall State/USAID services contract obligations, with the share of State/USAID services contract obligations awarded under multiple-award IDCs falling from 45 percent in 2009 to 34 percent in 2012. FSS and other IDVs (0.6 percent 3-year CAGR) were mostly stagnant, while definitive contracts (3.5 percent 3-year CAGR) and single-award IDCs (5.4 percent 3-year CAGR) showed moderate growth even as overall State/USAID services contract obligations declined. The share of State/USAID services contract obligations awarded under definitive contracts rose from 31 percent in 2009 to 37 percent in 2012, while the share awarded under single-award IDCs rose from 11 percent in 2009 to 15 percent in 2012.

Between 2011 and 2012, there were declines in the shares of State/USAID services contract obligations awarded under both single-award IDCs (17 percent to 15 percent) and multiple-award IDCs (37 percent to 34 percent). The share awarded under definitive contracts rose from 33 percent to 37 percent, while the share awarded under FSS or other IDVs rose from 9 percent to 10 percent. The share awarded under purchase orders held steady at 3 percent.

Vendor Size

In the 2009–2012 period, State/USAID services contract obligations awarded to both the Big 6 vendors (4.5 percent 3-year CAGR) and small vendors (6.3 percent 3-year CAGR) grew, even as overall State/USAID services contract obligations declined. State/USAID services contract obligations awarded to medium vendors (-1.9 percent 3-year CAGR) declined, though slower than the rate of decline for overall State/USAID services contract obligations. State/USAID services contract obligations awarded to large vendors declined sharply (-11.7 percent 3-year CAGR), falling as a share of overall State/USAID services contract obligations from 23 percent in 2009 to 20 percent in 2012.

Between 2011 and 2012, the share of State/USAID services contract obligations awarded to medium vendors rose from 59 percent to 63 percent. The Big 6 vendors also gained as a share of State/USAID services contract obligations, rising from 4 percent in 2009 to 5 percent in 2012. The share awarded to large vendors declined from 23 percent to 20 percent, while the share awarded to small vendors held steady at 13 percent.

Top 10

Only one vendor, Dyncorp International, was in the top 5 for State/USAID in both 2002 and 2012. Of the other four members of the top 5 in 2002 (Development Alternatives Group, Halliburton, Justin Paving, and Caddell Construction), only Development Alternatives Group remains in the top 20 in 2012. As a share of overall State/USAID services contract obligations, the top 5 declined from 35 percent in 2002 to 24 percent in 2012, while the top 10 declined from 44 percent in 2002 to 34 percent in 2012.

The top 5 vendors were largely unchanged between 2011 and 2012, with PFSCM (6th in 2011, 4th in 2012) replacing Triple Canopy (5th in 2011, 10th in 2012). Seven companies who were outside the top 20 in 2012 rose into the top 20 in 2012, an unusual amount of volatility: SAIC (24th in 2011, 7th in 2012), American International Vendors Special Projects (outside the top 100 in 2011, 9th in 2012), Black & Veatch (34th in 2011, 14th in 2012), AECOM Technology (25th in 2011, 16th in 2012), General Dynamics (71st in 2011, 17th in 2012), the Desbuild Incorporated Rec International joint venture (outside the top 100 in 2011, 18th in 2012), and Creative Associates International (32nd in 2011, 19th in 2012). Berger Group saw the largest decline between 2011 and 2012, falling from 11th in 2011 to 20th in 2012.

Figure 4-7: Services Contracting by NASA, 2000–2012

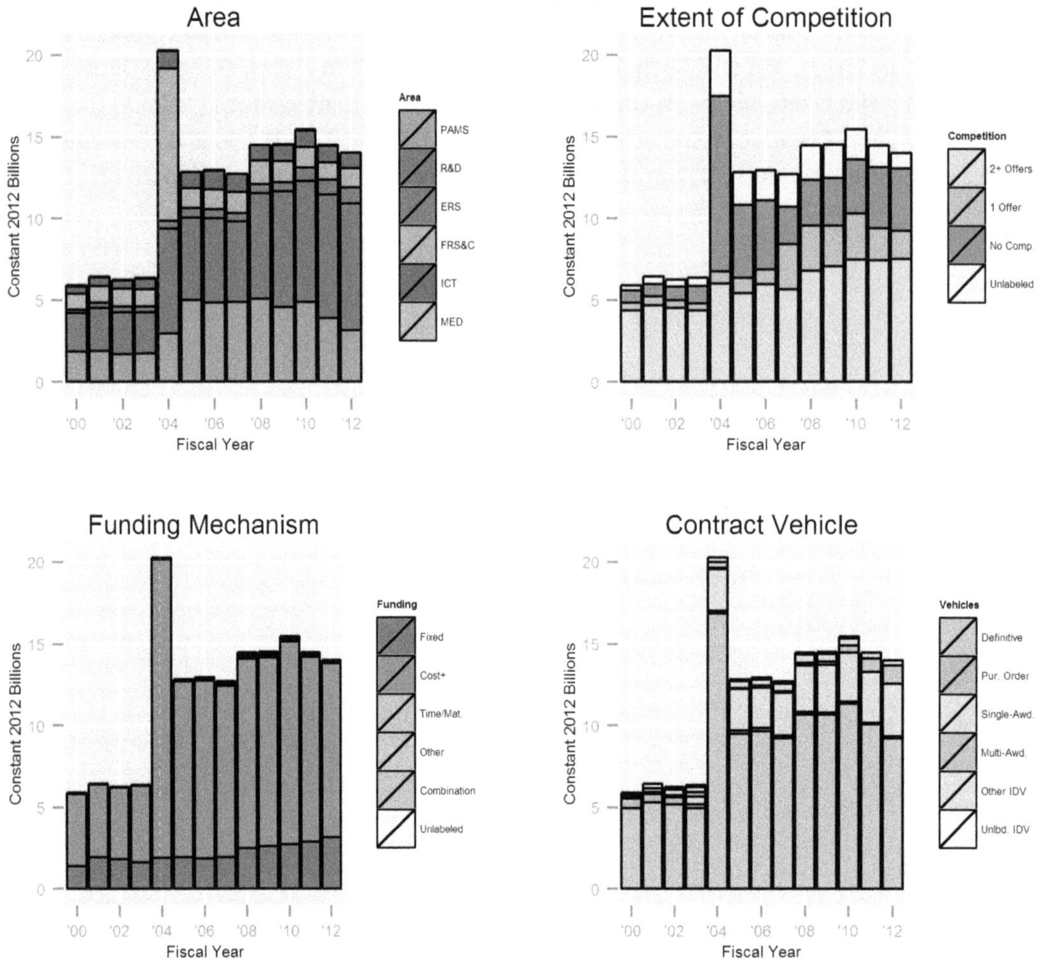

Top 10 Vendors

Vendor	2012 Millions	2011 Rank
California Institute of Technology	1,680	1
Lockheed Martin	1,450	2
Boeing	1,430	3
Jacobs Engineering Group	680	5
United Space Alliance*	630	4
Roscosmos	590	7
Orbital Sciences	370	10
Northrop Grumman	330	11
ATK	320	6
United Launch Services	310	8
Top 10 NASA Obligations	9,990	
Total NASA Obligations	14,020	

* Joint Venture

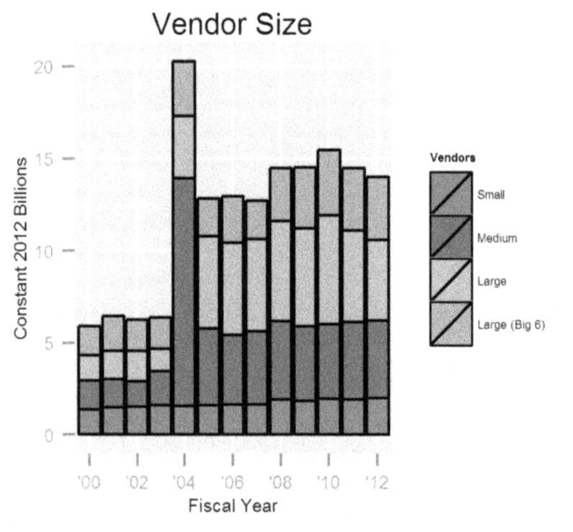

Source: FPDS; CSIS analysis.

NASA

Between 2000 and 2012, NASA's total obligations for services increased 139 percent from $5.9 billion to $14 billion. Over this period, R&D contract obligations increased over threefold, rising from a 40 percent share of contract obligations in 2000 to 55 percent in 2012. The share of NASA services contract obligations awarded after competition with multiple offers dropped from around 70 percent from 2000 to 2003 to 30 percent in 2004, but has slowly climbed since, to 54 percent in 2012. Over 70 percent of NASA services contract obligations have been awarded under fixed price contract types in every year during this period. Definitive contracts made up the majority of NASA's contract obligations over the last decade—peaking at 83 percent of service contract obligations in 2002; however, its share has since dropped to 66 percent in 2012, as single-award IDCs and multiple-award IDCs have become more common. Roughly equal shares of NASA services contract obligations were awarded across the four vendor size categories in the early 2000s, but small vendors have dropped off significantly since, while the share of contract obligations awarded to large vendors has grown.

In the 2009–2012 period, NASA services contract obligations declined at a -1.2 percent 3-year CAGR. Between 2011 and 2012, NASA services contract obligations declined by 3 percent.

Service Areas

In the 2009–2012 period, NASA services contract obligations awarded for ERS grew at a robust 19.6 percent 3-year CAGR. R&D, consistently the largest service area within NASA, grew at a 3.1 percent 3-year CAGR, evidence that NASA has managed to preserve contracts for core research functions even as contract obligations have declined. NASA ICT contract obligations (-1.4 percent 3-year CAGR) declined at a rate similar to that of overall NASA services contract obligations, while FRS&C (-3.3 percent 3-year CAGR), MED (-5.3 percent 3-year CAGR), and PAMS (-11.6 percent 3-year CAGR) declined faster than overall NASA services.

Between 2011 and 2012, R&D and ERS obligations increased by 1 percent and 3 percent, respectively. With the exception of ERS and FRS&C, which increased by 7 and 10 percent respectively in this period, obligations in all other service areas fell: PAMS (-19 percent) and ICT (-7 percent) both declined faster than overall NASA services, as did MED (-32 percent), although MED has not accounted for more than $50 million in any year since 2000.

Competition

In the 2009–2012 period, NASA services contract obligations awarded after competition with multiple offers grew at a 2.3 percent 3-year CAGR, even as overall NASA services contract obligations declined, rising as a share from 49 percent in 2009 to 54 percent in 2012. Unlike many other government agencies and service areas, however, limited competition with multiple offers (4.7 percent 3-year CAGR) did not drastically outgrow full competition with multiple offers (1.6 percent 3-year CAGR). Contract obligations awarded without competition grew at almost four times the rate (9.0 percent 3-year CAGR) of competition with multiple offers, rising as a share of overall NASA services contract obligations from 20 percent in 2009 to 27 percent in 2012. Contract obligations awarded after competition with a single offer (-11.8 percent 3-year CAGR) and unlabeled (-21.9 percent 3-year CAGR) both declined significantly during the period observed. As a share of overall NASA services contract obligations, competition with a single offer fell from 17 percent in 2009 to 12 percent in 2012, while unlabeled fell from 14 percent in 2009 to 7 percent in 2012.

Between 2011 and 2012, the share of NASA services contract obligations awarded after competition with multiple offers rose from 51 percent to 54 percent, while the share awarded without competition rose from 26 percent to 27 percent. Contract obligations awarded after competition with a single offer fell from 14 percent to 12 percent.

Funding Mechanism

In the 2009–2012 period, NASA services contract obligations awarded under fixed price contract type increased at 6.5 percent 3-year CAGR while overall NASA services contract obligations (1.2 percent 3-year CAGR), increasing as a share from 18 percent in 2009 to 22 percent in 2012. Contract obligations awarded under cost reimbursement contract types fell at a -2.7 percent 3-year CAGR, falling from 80 percent of NASA services contract obligations in 2009 to 76 percent in 2012. Contract obligations awarded under time and materials declined at a rate (-1.5 percent 3-year CAGR) similar to overall NASA services, but never exceeded $150 million in any given year. Combination and unlabeled contracts were never a major factor in NASA services contracting, to their credit.

Between 2011 and 2012, the share of NASA services contract obligations awarded under fixed price contract types rose from 20 percent to 22 percent, while the share awarded under cost reimbursement contract types fell from 78 percent to 76 percent.

Contract Vehicle

In the 2009–2012 period, NASA services contract obligations awarded under definitive contracts (-4.6 percent 3-year CAGR) fell somewhat faster than overall NASA services, declining as a share of overall NASA services contract obligations from 73 percent in 2009 to 66 percent in 2012. Purchase orders (-10.2 percent 3-year CAGR) and FSS and other IDVs (-13.1 percent 3-year CAGR) both declined significantly, but neither is a major factor in NASA services contracting. Single-award IDCs (3.0 percent 3-year CAGR) showed minor growth throughout the period, while multiple-award IDCs (80.8 percent 3-year CAGR) have grown explosively, rising from just 1 percent of contract obligations in 2009 to 8 percent in 2012.

Between 2011 and 2012, the share of NASA services contract obligations awarded under definitive contracts fell from 70 percent to 66 percent. Single-award IDCs rose from 22 percent to 23 percent, while multiple-award IDCs rose from 6 percent to 8 percent. Purchase orders and FSS and other IDVs held steady at 1 percent and 2 percent, respectively.

Vendor Size

In the 2009–2012 period, NASA services contract obligations awarded to small vendors grew at a 2.4 percent 3-year CAGR. Medium vendors (1.3 percent 3-year CAGR) and the Big 6 vendors (1.2 percent 3-year CAGR) grew, even as overall NASA services contract obligations declined. Contract obligations awarded to large vendors saw moderate decline during the period (-6.1 percent 3-year CAGR), declining as a share of overall NASA services contract obligations from 37 percent in 2009 to 31 percent in 2012.

Between 2011 and 2012, the share of NASA services contract obligations awarded to small vendors rose from 13 percent to 14 percent, medium vendors grew from 29 percent to 30 percent, and the Big 6 vendors rose from 23 percent to 25 percent. The share awarded to large vendors declined from 34 percent to 31 percent.

Top 10

Three vendors in the top 5 NASA services vendors for 2002 were not in the top 10 for 2012: Johns Hopkins APL (19th in 2012), Space Gateway Support, and Raytheon (both outside the top 20 in 2012). They are replaced in the top 5 by the California Institute of Technology, Jacobs Engineering Group, and the United Space Alliance joint venture, none of which were in the top 20 in 2002. Unlike most other government agencies and service categories, NASA services contract obligations have become more concentrated among top vendors in the past decade. The share of NASA services contract obligations awarded to the top 5 rose from 34 percent in 2002 to 42 percent in 2012, while the share awarded to the top 10 rose from 46 percent to 56 percent.

The top 5 NASA services vendors are largely unchanged from 2011 to 2012. Two companies that were outside the top 20 in 2011 rose into the top 20 in 2012: Johns Hopkins APL (22nd in 2011, 19th in 2012) and General Dynamics (25th in 2011, 20th in 2012). The only vendor to fall out of the top 10 between 2011 and 2012 was United Technologies (9th in 2011, 13th in 2012), replaced by Northrop Grumman (11th in 2011, 8th in 2012.)

Figure 4-8: Services Contracting by Other Agencies, 2000–2012

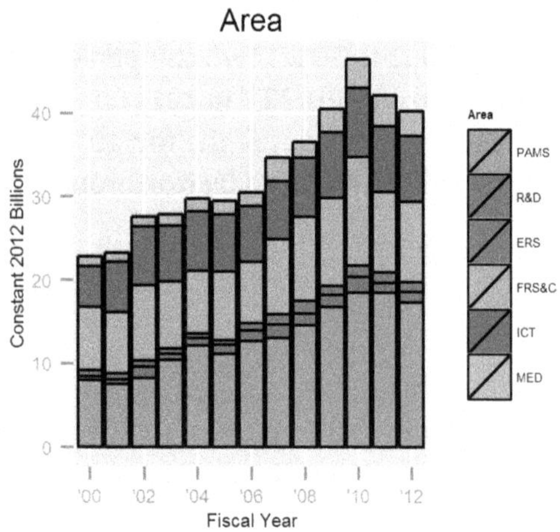

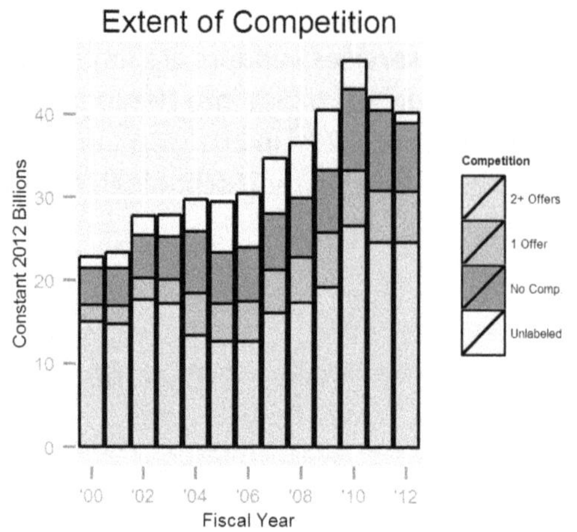

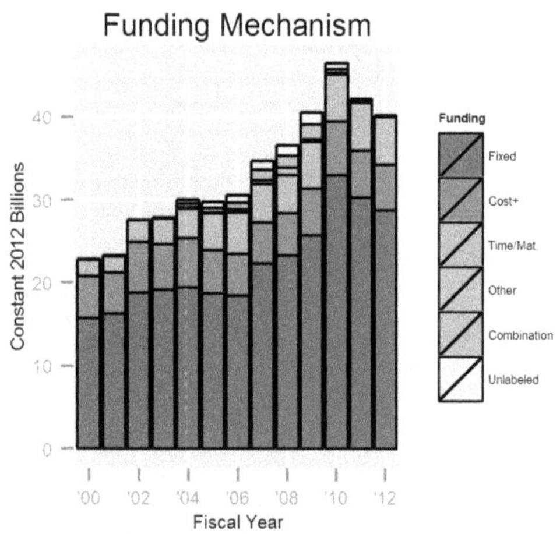

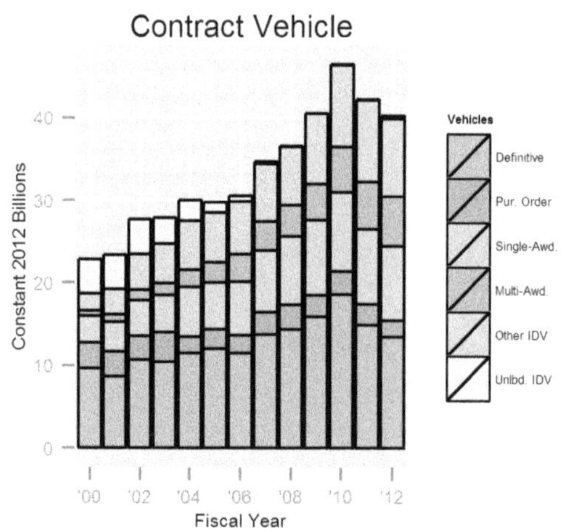

Top 10 Vendors

Vendor	2012 Millions	2011 Rank
Lockheed Martin	1,030	1
Booz Allen Hamilton	770	2
Harris	620	10
Kiewit-Turner Joint Venture*	580	--
Computer Sciences Corp.	450	4
Deloitte	440	13
Accenture	390	12
IBM	380	5
MTC	350	3
CCA	330	11
Top 10 Other Obligations	8,270	
Total Other Obligations	40,240	

* Joint Venture

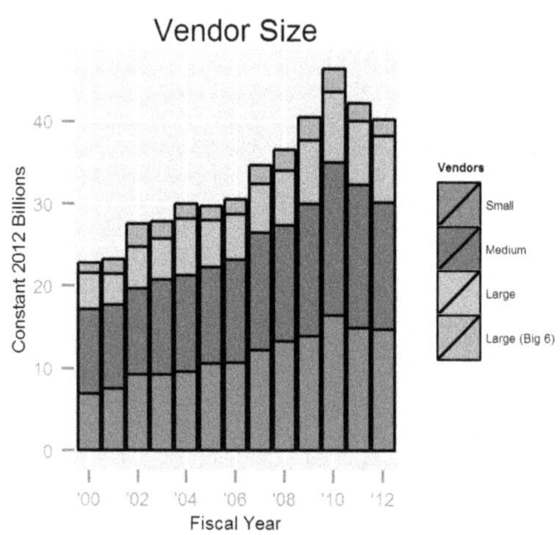

Source: FPDS; CSIS analysis.

Other Agencies

This section includes the consolidation of the federal government agencies whose obligations did not meet our threshold for individual breakout and analysis. Because of the degree of aggregation, the overall trends described in this section should not be assumed to apply to any particular individual entity.

PAMS remained the largest service area for these other departments, rarely dipping below 40 percent of total contract dollars after 2004. The share of services contract obligations for other agencies awarded after competition with multiple offers was over 60 percent from 2000 to 2003, but dropped below 50 percent from 2004 to 2009, before rebounding to 61 percent in 2012. Fixed price remained the preferred funding mechanism for service contracts in all other departments, never falling below 60 percent of contract obligations throughout the last 13 years. Definitive contracts were the most common contract vehicle among other agencies throughout the period observed, accounting for nearly 40 percent in every year until 2011. Nearly 40 percent of services contract obligations for other agencies were awarded to medium vendors in most years, with small vendors accounting for nearly 35 percent in most years.

In the 2009–2012 period, services contract obligations for other agencies were mostly stagnant (-0.2 percent 3-year CAGR). Between 2011 and 2012, services contract obligations for other agencies declined by 5 percent.

Note that services contract obligations by other agencies were temporarily inflated in 2009 and 2010 due to the American Recovery and Reinvestment Act (ARRA) of 2009, which accounted for 5 percent of services contract obligations by other agencies in 2009 and 9 percent in 2010. See Chapter 5 for further discussion of the impact of ARRA on services contract trends.

Service Areas

In the 2009–2012 period, ICT (0.0 percent 3-year CAGR) and PAMS (1.0 percent 3-year CAGR) closely tracked the overall rate of change for other agencies. MED (1.8 percent 3-year CAGR) and ERS (4.6 percent 3-year CAGR) grew relative to overall services contract obligations for other agencies, while FRS&C (-2.9 percent 3-year CAGR) and R&D (-5.0 percent 3-year CAGR) showed moderate declines.

Between 2011 and 2012, none of the service areas changed more than 1 percent with the exception of MED, which experienced a 20 percent decline in contract obligated dollars, and PAMS, which fell by 6 percent.

Competition

In the 2009–2012 period, services contract obligations for other agencies awarded after competition with multiple offers grew at an 8.6 percent 3-year CAGR, rising as a share of overall services contract obligations for other agencies from 47 percent in 2009 to 61 percent in 2012. This growth was largely the product of a 17.2 percent 3-year CAGR for limited competition with multiple offers, which accounted for 52 percent of contract obligations awarded after competition with multiple offers in 2012, as well as better data labeling. Contract obligations awarded without competition grew more slowly (3.4 percent 3-year CAGR), rising as a share of overall services contract obligations for other agencies from 18 percent in 2009 to 20 percent in 2012. Contract obligations awarded after competition with a single offer declined slightly (-2.5 percent 3-year CAGR), while unlabeled, which had accounted for 18 percent of overall services contract obligations for other agencies in 2009, fell to 3 percent in 2012.

Between 2011 and 2012, the share of services contract obligations for other agencies awarded after competition with multiple offers rose from 58 percent to 61 percent. Competition with a single offer held steady at 15 percent, while services contract obligations for other agencies awarded without competition fell from23 percent to 20 percent.

Funding Mechanism

In the 2009–2012 period, services contract obligations for other agencies awarded under fixed price contract types grew at a 3.8 percent 3-year CAGR, rising as a share of overall services contract obligations for other agencies from 63 percent in 2009 to 72 percent in 2012, in part due to better data labeling. Services contract obligations for other agencies awarded under cost reimbursement contract types declined at a rate comparable to that of overall services contract obligations for other agencies (-1.5 percent 3-year CAGR), while contract obligations awarded under time and materials contracts showed slight growth (1.2 percent 3-year CAGR). Combination and unlabeled, neither of which ever individually accounted for more than 4 percent of services contract obligations for other agencies in any given year, each accounted for less than 1 percent in 2012.

Between 2011 and 2012, the share of services contract obligations for other agencies awarded under fixed price and time and materials contract types held steady at 72 percent and 14 percent, respectively. The share of services contract obligations for other agencies awarded under cost reimbursement contract types rose from 13 percent to 14 percent.

Contract Vehicle

In the 2009–2012 period, services contract obligations for other agencies awarded under definitive contracts declined faster than overall services contract obligations for other agencies (-5.5 percent 3-year CAGR), declining as a share of overall services contract obligations for other agencies from 39 percent in 2009 to 33 percent in 2012. Contract obligations awarded under purchase orders (-8.2 percent 3-year CAGR) declined even more steeply, while single-award IDCs (-0.4 percent 3-year CAGR) declined nearly in sync with overall services contract obligations for other agencies. FSS and other IDVs (3.6 percent 3-year CAGR) and multiple-award IDCs (11.4 percent 3-year CAGR) both saw growth, with multiple-award IDCs growing as a share of overall services contract obligations for other agencies from 11 percent in 2009 to 15 percent in 2012.

Between 2011 and 2012, the share of services contract obligations for other agencies awarded under definitive contracts declined from 35 percent to 33 percent, while purchase orders declined from 6 percent to 5 percent. Single-award IDCs rose from 21 percent to 22 percent, and multiple-award IDCs rose from 14 percent to 15 percent. The share of services contract obligations for other agencies awarded under FSS or other IDVs held steady at 23 percent.

Vendor Size

In the 2009–2012 period, services contract obligations for other agencies awarded to both small vendors (1.7 percent 3-year CAGR) and large vendors (1.2 percent 3-year CAGR) grew slightly, with the share of services contract obligations for other agencies awarded to small vendors rising from 34 percent in 2009 to 37 percent in 2012. Contract obligations awarded to medium vendors declined at a rate similar to that of overall services contract obligations for other agencies (-1.1 percent 3-year CAGR), while contract obligations awarded to large vendors declined sharply (-10.7 percent 3-year CAGR).

Between 2011 and 2012, the share of services contract obligations for other agencies awarded to small vendors rose from 35 percent to 37 percent, while the share awarded to large vendors rose from 18 percent to 20 percent. The share awarded to medium vendors declined from 41 percent to 39 percent, while the Big 6 vendors held steady at 5 percent.

Top 10

Four of the top 5 vendors for other agencies in 2002 were outside the top 5 in 2012: IBM (2nd in 2002, 8th in 2012), BAE Systems, Phoenix Marine, and Teltara (all outside the top 20 in 2012). Replacing them in the top 5 in 2012 were Booz Allen Hamilton, Harris, the Kiewet-Turner joint venture, and Computer Sciences Corp. The share of overall services contract obligations for other agencies awarded to the top 5 declined from 13 percent in 2002 to 9 percent in 2012, while the share awarded to the top 10 declined from 20 percent in 2009 to 13 percent in 2012.

There was moderate turnover in the top 5 between 2011 and 2012, with Harris (10th in 2011, 3rd in 2012) and the Kiewet-Turner joint venture (outside the top 100 in 2011, 4th in 2012) replacing IBM (5th in 2011, 8th in 2012) and Management & Training (3rd in 2011, 9th in 2012). Only one vendor outside the top 20 in 2011 rose into the top 20 in 2012: General Dynamics, which rose from 23rd in 2011 to 19th in 2012. Raytheon saw the most notable decline, dropping from 8th in 2011 to 20th in 2012.

Cross-Agency Participation by the Overall Top 20 Federal Services Vendors

Table 4-1: Cross-Agency Participation by the Overall Top 20 Federal Services Vendors, 2002

	Vendor	Defense	DHS	Energy	GSA	HHS	NASA	Other Agencies	Total
1	Lockheed Martin	9,680	0	2,680	470	40	710	1,408	15,002
2	University of California	30	-	9,420	-	50	10	8	9,515
3	Boeing	7,490	-	20	10	0	530	2	8,050
4	Northrop Grumman	4,960	-	0	330	160	110	442	6,019
5	Raytheon	4,640	-	0	50	0	350	286	5,324
Subtotal for Top 5	-	**26,810**	**0**	**12,130**	**850**	**250**	**1,700**	**2,145**	**43,910**
6	General Dynamics	4,440	-	0	40	10	0	108	4,631
7	Bechtel	620	-	3,620	-	-	0	(3)	4,234
8	SAIC	2,450	-	40	530	430	110	332	3,902
9	ASDV	-	-	-	2,980	-	-	-	2,978
10	Dyncorp International	1,510	-	170	340	20	140	203	2,638
11	TRW	2,090	-	10	90	40	140	247	2,613
12	Computer Sciences Corp.	1,320	-	60	540	70	40	438	2,497
13	Health Net	2,120	-	-	-	-	-	5	2,122
14	BAE Systems	1,200	-	-	170	0	10	545	1,957
15	Acepex Management	20	10	-	1,830	0	-	1	1,853
16	United Technologies	1,700	-	-	0	-	70	11	1,777
17	Washington Savannah River Company*	-	-	1,780	-	-	-	-	1,776
18	Humana	1,630	-	-	-	-	-	-	1,633
19	Booz Allen Hamilton	850	-	30	180	60	20	235	1,397
20	Electronic Data Systems	570	-	40	210	40	0	477	1,337
Total for Top 20	-	**47,330**	**10**	**17,870**	**7,750**	**920**	**2,230**	**4,745**	**81,254**
Total for all industry	-	**118,760**	**30**	**29,510**	**20,470**	**7,100**	**6,250**	**27,620**	**214,877**

* Joint Venture

Source: FPDS; CSIS analysis. All figures in 2012 millions.

Table 4-2: Cross-Agency Participation by the Overall Top 20 Federal Services Vendors, 2012

	Vendor		Defense	DHS	Energy	GSA	HHS	NASA	Other Agencies	Total
1	Lockheed Martin		11,570	400	2,620	230	310	1,450	1,030	17,970
2	Boeing		8,350	50	0	10	0	1,430	20	9,850
3	Northrop Grumman		7,990	130	0	230	250	330	320	9,260
4	SAIC		4,480	280	20	600	590	260	280	6,760
5	Raytheon		6,080	30	0	0	0	60	260	6,430
Subtotal for Top 5		-	**38,470**	**900**	**2,640**	**1,060**	**1,150**	**3,520**	**1,910**	**50,280**
6	General Dynamics		3,240	190	20	210	250	170	260	4,500
7	L3 Communications		3,780	120	10	80	0	50	190	4,350
8	Booz Allen Hamilton		2,570	160	40	300	170	30	770	4,040
9	Computer Sciences Corp.		2,250	670	30	40	140	200	450	3,900
10	Dyncorp International		2,790	-	20	0	50	30	10	3,540
11	Humana		3,470	-	-	-	-	-	10	3,470
12	URS		1,960	40	1,100	100	0	220	60	3,470
13	Bechtel		1,630	-	1,670	-	-	-	-	3,300
14	Health Net		2,930	-	-	-	-	-	210	3,140
15	BAE Systems		2,900	50	0	60	0	10	90	3,110
16	TriWest Healthcare		3,010	-	-	-	-	-	-	3,010
17	Battelle		490	50	1,640	10	80	0	20	2,290
18	CACI		1,880	40	0	130	0	0	220	2,270
19	Hewlett-Packard		1,330	190	0	180	130	90	300	2,220
20	ITT		1,850	0	-	0	-	150	220	2,200
Total for Top 20		-	**74,550**	**2,410**	**7,180**	**2,150**	**1,960**	**4,470**	**4,700**	**99,100**
Total for all industry		-	**186,760**	**9,640**	**24,380**	**7,350**	**13,820**	**14,020**	**40,240**	**307,750**

Source: FPDS; CSIS analysis. All figures in 2012 millions.

Between 2002 and 2012, the government agency participation of the top 5 federal services vendors has not diversified significantly. DoE contract obligations in the top 5 have dropped significantly, largely due to changes in contract awards for management of the national nuclear laboratories, but contract obligations for every other government agency except "other agencies" have increased significantly. The top 5 are even more heavily weighted toward DoD in 2012 than they were in 2002, with over 77 percent of top 5 contract obligations awarded to DoD in 2012, compared to 61 percent in 2002. The same holds true for the top 20, where 75 percent of contract obligations were awarded to DoD in 2012, compared with 58 percent in 2002.

DoE had the largest share of its services contract obligations concentrated in the overall top 20 services vendors in 2002 (61 percent), but that share declined to 29 percent in 2012. DoD remained steady, with the overall top 20 accounting for 40 percent of overall DoD services contract obligations in both 2002 and 2012. HHS (13 percent in 2002, 14 percent in 2012) and State/USAID (8 percent in 2002, 15 percent in 2012) were the least concentrated agencies in terms of shares of services contract obligations awarded to the overall top 20 services vendors.

Chapter 5: Policy Implications

The U.S. government is spending less on services, multi-award vehicles have become more prevalent, unlabeled and contradictory data is becoming rarer, and the rate of competition has declined. These trends, and the many others covered in prior chapters, provide a necessary foundation for addressing policy questions. However, discussing the key questions raised by policymakers, the concerns of overworked policymakers, and the complaints of vendors typically touch on multiple contract characteristics. The research team has chosen five such questions to explore based on their relevance to current debates:

- **Has the rise of multiple-award IDCs in federal services contracting reduced competition?**
- **How does level of competition vary by size of contract?**
- **Is there a "mid-tier squeeze" in federal services contracting?**
- **What effect did the American Recovery and Reinvestment Act of 2009 (ARRA) have on federal services contracting trends?**
- **Has data quality improved since 2010, and what new data quality issues have appeared since?**

This research touches on issues that technical limitations prevented the study team from examining in prior reports. As is discussed in the methodology section (Chapter 1), this is the first iteration of the report that combines all federal contracting data into a single database including all available columns. This integration allowed the study team to improve our large vendor classifications and for the first time to cross-tabulate contract vehicle with the other variables. The purpose of this work was to make it possible to address questions of interest to our audience with greater fidelity and depth than in our past reports.

Future versions of this report will take on new questions, and will incorporate these lessons into the team's understanding of our traditional contract categories. Much of this research was driven by questions from attendees at our events, contracting practitioners, fellow observers, and vendors. We are grateful to all who contributed questions and look forward to suggestions of where we should go next.

Has the rise of multiple-award IDCs in federal services contracting reduced competition?

As discussed in Chapter 2, the share of federal services contract obligations awarded under multiple-award IDCs has more than tripled, from 6 percent in 2000 to 20 percent in 2012. Under FAR 16.504(c), contracting officers are directed to give preference to multiple awards for indefinite delivery contracts, when appropriate and practicable. Largely as a result of the rise of multiple-award contracts, growth in limited competition with multiple offers (52.1 percent 12-year CAGR) has more than quadrupled growth in full competition with multiple offers (12.7 percent 12-year CAGR) between 2000 and 2012. During the same period, limited competition with multiple offers has grown as a share of overall services contract obligations awarded after competition with multiple offers from 23 percent in 2000 to 43 percent in 2012. On its face, this is a worrisome trend, but deeper analysis shows that, **though competition under multiple-award IDCs may in fact be "limited," the federal government still largely receives the benefits of competition under multiple-award IDCs.**

CSIS classifies contract awards under multiple-award IDCs as "limited competition" because only approved vendors in the multiple award are able to compete. This is mitigated by the fact that the process to become an approved vendor under a multiple-award IDC is (in theory) open to any qualified party, and that contracting officers are required under the FAR to make any contract action over $3,000 under a multiple-award IDC available to any vendor participating in the multiple award, subject to certain exceptions (such as urgency, follow-on, and single source). In 2012, only 7 percent of federal services contract obligations awarded under multiple-award IDCs were awarded without competition, far lower than the rates for definitive contracts (27 percent), single-award IDCs (30 percent), FSS or other IDVs (24 percent), or purchase orders (47 percent).

Figure 5-1 shows, for services contract obligations that were competed, how many offers were received for the different types of contract vehicles:

Figure 5-1: Number of Offers Received for Competed Federal Services Contract Obligations, by Contract Vehicle, 2012

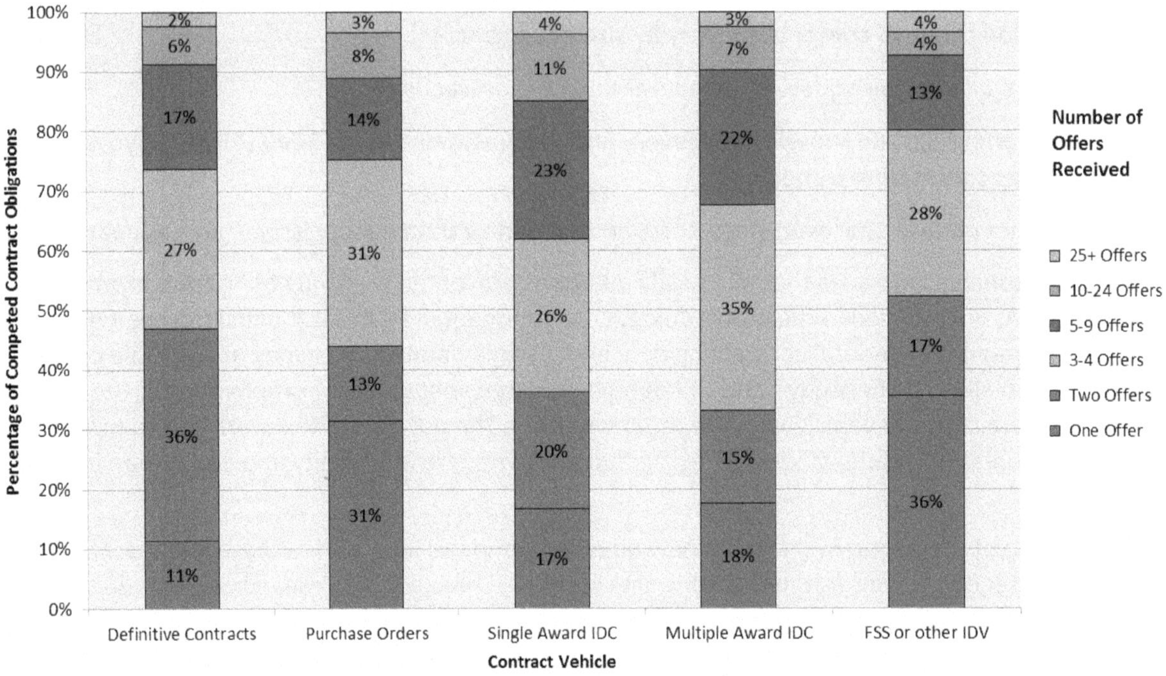

Source: FPDS; CSIS analysis.

In 2012, 67 percent of competed services contract obligations awarded under multiple-award IDCs received at least 3 offers, significantly higher than for single-award IDCs (64 percent), definitive contracts (53 percent), purchase orders (56 percent), or FSS or other IDVs (48 percent). The share of competed services contract obligations awarded under multiple-award IDCs receiving at least 5 offers was 32 percent in 2012, higher than for any other contract vehicle type except single-award IDCs (38 percent). **Curiously, for competed services contract obligations receiving only a single offer, the shares for multiple-award IDCs (18 percent) and single-award IDCs (17 percent) were very similar, and both were notably higher than for definitive contracts (11 percent).** Given that vendors under multiple-award IDCs are preapproved as capable of performing the specified functions, and are presumably motivated to win awards under the contract, it would be expected that fewer contract actions under multiple-award IDCs would receive only one offer. This suggests that some solicitations within multiple-award IDCs may be written in such a way that discourages some vendors from bidding. CSIS urges policymakers to examine why such a large percentage of multiple-award IDC contract obligations are awarded after receiving only one offer.

How does level of competition vary by size of contract?

In 2012, there was a clear trend in the share of services contract obligations awarded without competition when broken down by size of contract. Contract obligations for contracts from $5–$25 million (19 percent) and from $25–$100 million (20 percent) showed the lowest rates of "no competition." $1–$5 million contracts and contracts greater than $500 million showed slightly higher rates of awards without competition (24 percent for both). Contracts between $250,000 and $1 million (28 percent), contracts from $100–$500 million (30 percent), and contracts less than $250,000 (31 percent) showed the highest shares awarded without competition. Unsurprisingly, no competition (only one source) accounted for a larger share of contract obligations awarded without competition in larger contracts than in smaller contracts: only 33 percent of uncompeted contracts from $1–$5 million cited the "only one source" exception, compared to 52 percent for $5–$25 million, 61 percent for $25–$100 million, 58 percent for $100–$500 million, and 66 percent for contracts greater than $500 million.

Figure 5-2 shows the number of offers received in FY 2012 for competed contract obligations, broken down by size of contract:

Figure 5-2: Number of Offers Received for Competed Federal Services Contract Obligations, by Size of Contract, 2012

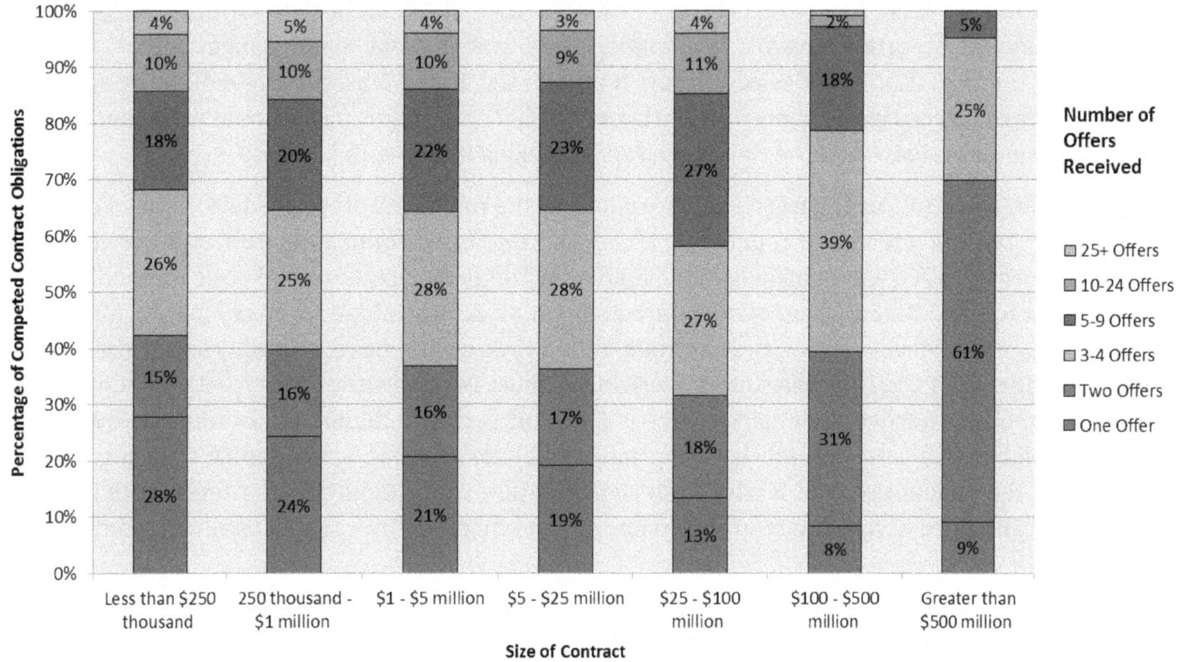

Source: FPDS; CSIS analysis.

The most striking aspect of this data breakdown is that 61 percent of competed contract obligations over $500 million are awarded with only 2 offers, 3–4 times the rate of any other contract size category except $100–$500 million (31 percent). Similarly, only 30 percent of competed contract obligations for contracts greater than $500 million received 3 or more offers, half the rate of every other size category. While the scope and complexity of some of these greater than $500 million services contracts (such as for management of the national nuclear laboratories) may be irreducible, the disproportionately large share of competed contracts greater than $500 million receiving only 2 offers indicates that there may be room for improvement in writing solicitations and/or contracts to bring in additional offerors.

Also notable is that there is a clear trend of the share of competed contract obligations awarded with only a single offer increasing as contract size decreases. Twenty-eight percent of competed contract obligations for contracts less than $250,000 received only a single offer, compared to 24 percent for $250,000–$1 million, 21 percent for $1–$5 million, 19 percent for contracts from $5–$25 million, 13 percent for $25–$100 million, 8 percent for $100–$500 million, and 9 percent for greater than $500 million. In all cases, there appears to be significant room to improve the quality of competition for federal services contracts by attracting additional bidders, either through better publicizing of contract solicitations, easing of barriers to entry in federal contracting, or improving solicitation/contract writing to remove disincentives to offerors.

Is there a "mid-tier squeeze" in federal services contracting?

As discussed in Chapter 2, **the share of services contract obligations awarded to medium vendors has been relatively stable between 2000 and 2012**, hovering between 28 and 31 percent. In recent years, services contract obligations awarded to medium vendors have declined at a rate (-4.5 percent 3-year CAGR) nearly identical to the overall rate of decline for services contract obligations (-4.7 percent 3-year CAGR). While some government agencies (such as DHS) have seen declines in contract obligations faster than their overall rates of decline from 2009 to 2012, others have seen growth (significant growth, in the case of DoE for government agencies). Of the service areas, only contract obligations awarded to medium vendors for FRS&C have declined faster than the overall rate of decline for the service area. This finding has two important caveats: first, market share stability may mask changes within the middle tier, which by our definition includes all vendors that with less than $3 billion in revenue that are not classified as small businesses. Second, FPDS data only reliably reports prime contract work, and thus the study team cannot evaluate whether large vendors are taking more work in-house.

It is beyond the scope of this report to evaluate whether the mid-tier's present equilibrium value is too low. That said, the study team has repeatedly heard a series of two complaints from mid-tier vendors: that certain forms of IDCs were challenging to vendors without the economies of scale to handle complex contracts and that mid-tier vendors are at an unfair disadvantage when competing for large contracts. Figure 5-3 shows that in 2012 **multiple-award IDCs do not have a notably lower share of medium vendors than does the market as a whole**. Medium vendors accounted for 31 percent of contract obligations awarded under single-award IDCs, compared to 29 percent for multiple-award IDCs. On the other hand, BOA and FSS, which we typically aggregate under FSS or other IDVs, do seem more welcoming to the middle-tier. This is true to an even greater extent to purchase orders, which have been notably in decline since before the study period began and might be one source of vendor complaints.

Figure 5-3: Vendor Size for Federal Services Contract Obligations, by Contract Vehicle, 2012

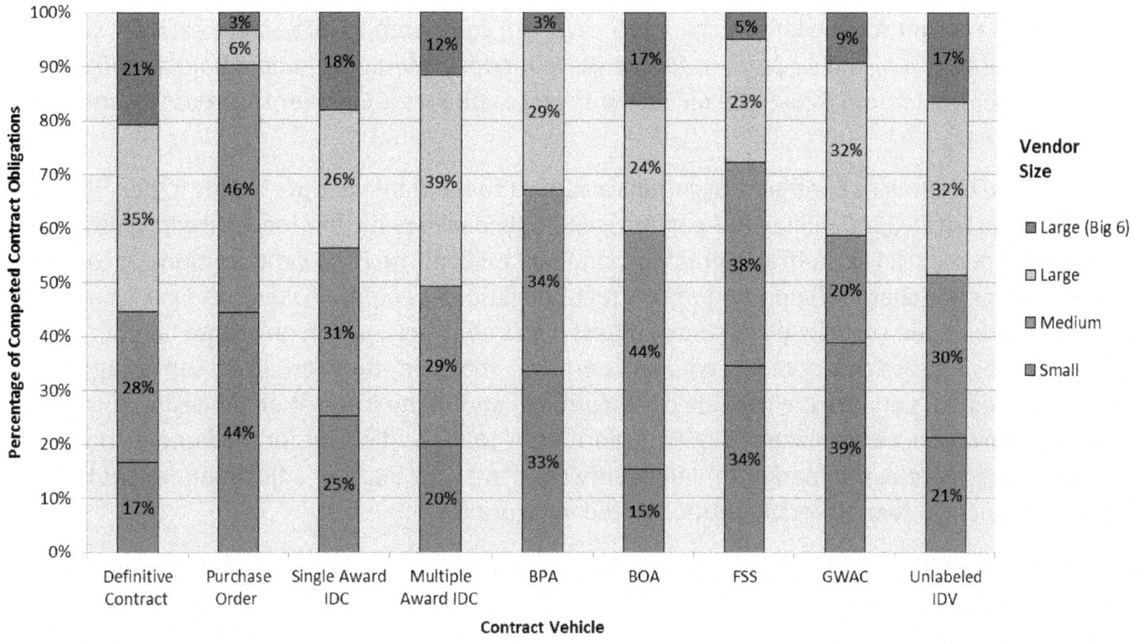

Source: FPDS; CSIS analysis.

The results were far more decisive when looking at annual contract size. **Large contracts put medium vendors at a significant disadvantage**. Figure 5-4 shows the share of FY 2012 services contract obligations awarded by vendor size, broken down further by size of annual contract obligations:

Figure 5-4: Vendor Size for Federal Services Contract Obligations, by Size of Contract, 2012

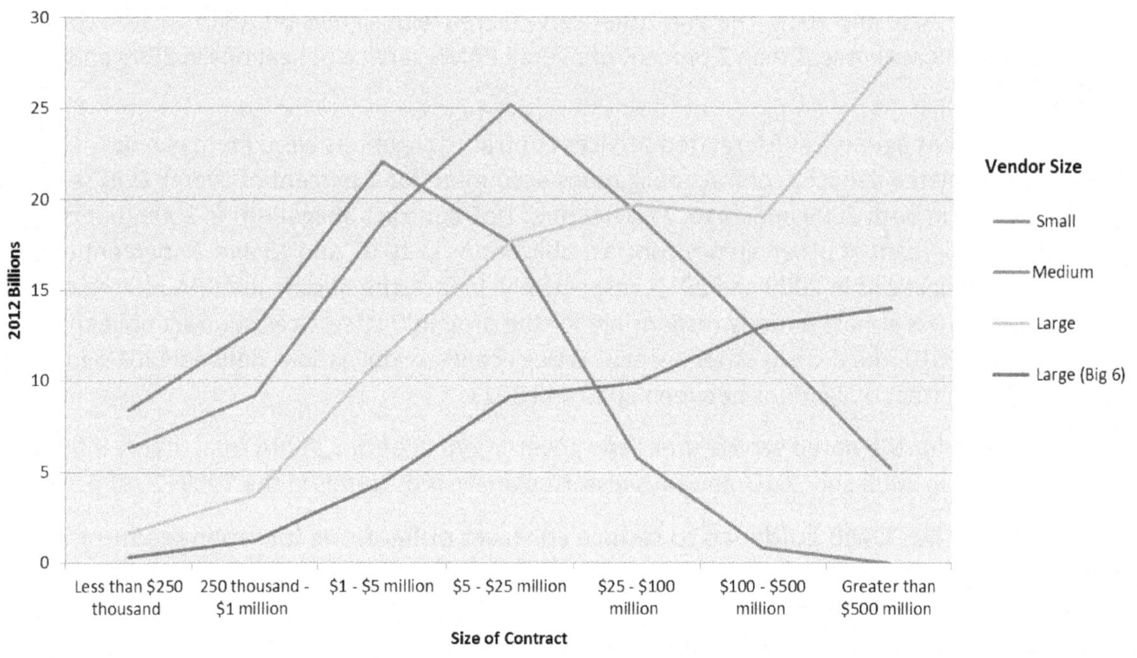

Source: FPDS; CSIS analysis.

For contracts under $5 million, small vendors and medium vendors account for the largest and second-largest shares of federal services contract obligations, respectively. For vendors from $5–$25 million, medium vendors account for the largest share (36 percent), compared to 25 percent each for small vendors and large vendors, and 13 percent for the Big 6 vendors. Medium vendors hold a similar share (35 percent) of contracts from $25–$100 million, with large vendors (36 percent) surpassing small vendors (11 percent).

The share of services contract obligations awarded to medium vendors begins to decline sharply for contracts from $100–$500 million (27 percent), and only declines further for contracts greater than $500 million (11 percent). For contracts greater than $500 million, the Big 6 vendors alone account for almost three times the share (30 percent) of contract obligations as medium vendors. One factor in this disparity is the scope and complexity of some large services contracts, which only large vendors have the necessary resources to compete for, win, and perform. That said, there are likely some larger contracts that medium vendors are capable of performing, and in the interest of increasing competition and spurring innovation, policymakers should explore ways to make it easier for medium vendors to meaningfully participate in the market for larger services contracts. Such an adjustment might help address the reliance on two offer competition noted in Figure 5-2.

What effect did the American Recovery and Reinvestment Act of 2009 (ARRA) have on federal services contracting trends?

In 2009 and 2010, 5 percent of overall federal services contract obligations ($16.6 billion in 2009, $16.1 billion in 2010) were tied to ARRA. **Services contract obligations tied to ARRA largely disappeared in 2011, and this decline accounted for nearly three-fourths of the overall decline in federal services contract obligations between 2010 and 2011**. Similarly, FRS&C contract obligations tied to ARRA accounted for 12 percent of overall FRS&C contract obligations in 2009 and 2010 ($13.7 billion in 2009, $12.2 billion in 2010). When ARRA-related FRS&C contract obligations largely disappeared between 2010 and 2011, this accounted for nearly three-quarters of the decline in overall FRS&C contract obligations between 2010 and 2011. The only other service area with significant ARRA-related contract obligations was PAMS, where less than 2 percent of overall PAMS service obligations in 2009 and 2010 were ARRA related.

By government agency, ARRA-related services contract obligations were more evenly distributed. ARRA-related services contract obligations accounted for 2 percent of overall DoD services contract obligations in both 2009 and 2010, 22 percent of DoE contract obligations in 2009 (but only 4 percent in 2010), 9 percent of other agency contract obligations in 2010, and 13 and 24 percent of GSA services contract obligations in 2009 and 2010, respectively. In fact, the decline in ARRA-related contract obligations after 2010 is almost entirely responsible for the drop in DoE services contract obligations between 2009 and 2010, the drop in other agency services contract obligations between 2010 and 2011, and GSA services contract obligations between 2010 and 2011.

Overall, and for the noted service areas and government agencies, ARRA temporarily inflated contract obligations in 2009 and 2010, and thus distorted analysis of trends in the 2009–2012 period.

How much impact has OMB guidance to reduce contract obligations for "management support services" had?

On November 7, 2011, OMB issued a guidance memorandum calling for a 15 percent reduction in contract obligations for 12 PSC codes[7] that fall under ICT and PAMS. Table 5-1 shows the results, broken down by government agency:

Table 5-1: Federal Contract Obligations for Management Support Services, 2010–2012

Agency	FY2010	FY2011	FY2012
Defense	26.12	24.83	22.91
DHS	2.06	1.93	1.43
Energy	0.59	0.40	0.42
GSA	1.08	1.45	1.30
HHS	1.24	1.20	1.07
NASA	3.44	2.76	2.14
Other Agencies	4.59	4.26	3.98
State and USAID	3.46	3.58	3.26
Total	**42.58**	**40.41**	**36.51**

Source: FPDS; CSIS analysis. All figures in 2012 billions.

In aggregate, the OMB goal was not met, as contract obligations for management support services declined by only 10 percent between 2011 and 2012, from $40.4 billion to $36.5 billion. Most agencies saw declines similar to the overall rate of decline, except for DoE, which saw 5 percent growth in management support services contract obligations between 2011 and 2012. **However, DHS (26 percent reduction, from $1.9 billion to $1.4 billion) and NASA (22 percent reduction, from $2.8 billion to $2.1 billion) were notable exceptions that surpassed OMB's targeted reductions.**

By PSC code, most of the decline in contract obligations for management support services was in R414 (Systems Engineering Services), which dropped from $4.2 billion in 2011 to $1.9 billion in 2012, and R421 (Technical Assistance), which dropped from $3.6 billion in 2011 to $2.3 billion in 2012. These two codes were eliminated and merged into R425 (Engineering and Technical Services), however, so there should technically be no obligations under either code for 2012. R425 was virtually unchanged in 2012 ($17.5 billion in 2012, from $17.2 billion in 2011), which indicates that there was a real reduction in obligations in some combination of those three codes between 2011 and 2012, although the data does not allow a specific conclusion as to which of those three categories of services saw real reductions in contract obligations.

Has data quality improved since 2010, and what new data quality issues have appeared since?

Overall, **data quality in FPDS has improved dramatically in recent years**. As recently as 2005, 9 percent of federal services contract obligations were unlabeled with regards to level of competition. By 2010, only 4 percent were unlabeled, and in 2012 only 2 percent were unlabeled. For funding mechanism, unlabeled has not exceeded 2 percent since 2002, but combination contracts (which include both fixed price and cost reimbursement elements) accounted for 10 percent of federal services contract obligations in 2009. That number fell to 2 percent in 2010, and dropped down to 1 percent in 2012. DoD, which accounts for the largest share of services contract obligations, had less than 1 percent of its contract obligations unlabeled for level of competition. The rate for other most government agencies is higher: 7 percent for NASA, 5 percent for DHS and GSA, and 4 percent for DoE and HHS. Nonetheless, all

[7] Two of those codes, R414 (Systems Engineering Services) and R421 (Technical Assistance), were eliminated and merged into a third management support services code, R425 (Engineering and Technical Services), for FY 2012 in the August 2011 update to the FPDS PSC Manual.

of these government agencies except DoE have seen significant declines in the shares of services contract obligations unlabeled for level of competition.

Also on the issue of data entry, the August 2011 revision of the FPDS PSC Manual made some significant changes, completely replacing the coding system for a number of services code letters (mostly related to FRS&C). This change was supposed to go into effect for FY 2012, with agencies switching over to the new codes, but the results have been less than encouraging. In 2012, 96 percent of contract obligations under service code M ($20.7 billion total in 2012) are labeled using the old coding system. Similarly, 60 percent of contract obligations under service code X ($530 million total in 2012[8]) and 20 percent of contract obligations under service codes Y and Z ($24.6 billion and $13.3 billion total in 2012, respectively) are labeled using the old coding system. This problem seems to be federal government-wide, rather than restricted to any particular agency or agencies. This data issue has the potential to cause serious confusion if users attempt trend analysis by PSC code or category.

As discussed in Chapter 4, there is a serious issue with GSA's FPDS submissions. GSA services contract obligations declined from $11.3 billion in 2011 to $7.2 billion in 2012, a 37 percent decrease, almost entirely in FRS&C. The primary driver of this decline is GSA's decision to cease reporting "lease and supplemental lease agreements for real property" to FPDS because such submissions are not mandated by in FAR 4.606(b)(3). While there is no legal requirement, **the decision to stop reporting contracts for lease of office buildings into FPDS represents a large step backwards for data transparency.** Study team estimates using FY 2010 values suggests that in FY 2012, **these leases could represent 39 percent of GSA's total services contract obligations, and 1.5 percent of total federal services contract obligations.**

This missing data is dwarfed by the underreporting of subcontracting data, which began being reported to FPDS in significant quantities starting in 2011. The office of the Deputy Assistant Secretary of Defense for Manufacturing and Industrial base estimates that 70 percent of DoD obligations now go through subcontractors.[9] However, in both 2011 and 2012, the total sub-award amount for DoD is less than 10 percent of DoD's total obligations. This means that **the vast majority of DoD sub-award dollars go unreported**. At present, the study team does not have estimates of subcontracting rates specific to services contracting or for the remainder of the government. The authors intend to determine and publicize the exact scope of this problem in future reports.

During the course of this research effort, the study team has noted that the USAspending.gov team makes frequent changes to the data structure of the FPDS data, but only publishes notification of such changes on an annual basis, if that frequently. This has led to significant difficulty for the study team and for other users of FPDS data in the past, especially in instances where the changes to the data structure have introduced major data errors (such as all data on small business determinations being wiped out.) A regularly updated change log would alleviate this issue, and allow regular data users to provide rapid feedback to the USAspending.gov team on bugs and data errors.

The study team urges policy makers in Congress, in government-wide oversight agencies such as OMB, and within contracting agencies to give attention to these issues going forward.

---

[8] Total contract obligations for code X are artificially low, due to the removal of $4.7 billion of GSA contract obligations for lease of office buildings over the last two years.

[9] Zachary Fryer-Biggs, "Interview: Brett Lambert, U.S. Defense Department's Industrial Policy," *Defense News*, December 18, 2012, http://mobile.defensenews.com/article/312180011.

Appendix: Service Area Classification of Product or Service Codes (PSCs)

Product or Service Code	CSIS Service Category
A - Research & Development	PAMS and R&D
B - Special Studies & Analyses - Not R&D	PAMS
C - Architect & Engineering - Construction	PAMS
D - Automatic Data Processing & Telecommunication	ICT
E - Purchase of Structures & Facilities	FRS&C
F - Natural Resources & Conservation	FRS&C
G - Social Services	MED
H - Quality Control, Testing, & Inspection	ICT and PAMS
J - Maintenance, Repair, & Rebuilding of Equipment	ERS and ICT
K - Modification of Equipment	ERS and ICT
L - Technical Representitive	ICT and PAMS
M - Operation of Government Owned Facilities	FRS&C
N - Installation of Equipment	ERS and ICT
P - Salvage Services	ERS and FRS&C
Q - Medical Services	MED
R - Professional, Administrative, & Management Support	PAMS
S - Utilities & Housekeeping Services	FRS&C and ICT
T - Photographic, Mapping, Printing, & Publications	PAMS
U - Education & Training	PAMS
V - Transportation, Travel & Relocation	ERS and PAMS
W - Lease or Rental of Equipment	ERS and ICT
X -Lease or Rental of Facilities	FRS&C
Y - Construction of Structures & Facilities	FRS&C
Z - Maintenance, Repair, or Alteration of Real Property	FRS&C

About the Authors

David Berteau is senior vice president and director of the International Security Program at CSIS, covering national security strategy, policy, programs, and resources as well as defense management, contracting, and acquisition. He also directs the Defense-Industrial Initiatives Group, which assesses national security economics and industry. Mr. Berteau is an adjunct professor at Georgetown University and at the Lyndon B. Johnson School of Public Affairs, a director of the Procurement Round Table, and a fellow of the National Academy of Public Administration and the Robert S. Strauss Center at the University of Texas. Prior to joining CSIS, he was director of national defense and homeland security for Clark & Weinstock, director of Syracuse University's National Security Studies Program, and a senior vice president at Science Applications International Corporation (SAIC). He served at senior levels in the U.S. Defense Department under four defense secretaries, including four years as principal deputy assistant secretary of defense for production and logistics.

Guy Ben-Ari was a senior fellow and deputy director of the Defense-Industrial Initiatives Group at CSIS, where he worked on projects related to U.S. and European technology and industrial bases supporting defense. Prior to joining CSIS, Mr. Ben-Ari was a research associate at George Washington University's Center for International Science and Technology Policy, where he worked on European research and development policies and European network-centric capabilities. From 2000 to 2002, he conducted collaborative research and development programs for Gilat Satellite Networks Ltd. and from 1995 to 2000, he was a technology analyst for the Israeli government.

Gregory Sanders is a fellow with the Defense-Industrial Initiatives Group (DIIG) at CSIS, where he gathers and analyzes data on U.S. defense policy issues. He has worked on DIIG's software industrial base study and its complexity series. He previously worked as an intern for the CSIS Global Strategy Institute, where he focused on long-term global trends. Mr. Sanders holds an M.A. in international relations from the University of Denver and a B.A. in government and politics and a B.S. in computer science from the University of Maryland.

Jesse Ellman is a research associate with the Defense-Industrial Initiatives Group at CSIS. He specializes in U.S. defense acquisition policy, with a particular focus on recent U.S. Army modernization efforts, DoD cost estimation methodologies, and DoD and DHS contracting trends. Mr. Ellman holds a B.A. in political science from Stony Brook University and an M.A. with honors in security studies, with a concentration in military operations, from Georgetown University.

Andysheh Dadsetan is a research consultant with the Defense-Industrial Initiatives Group at CSIS, where he gathers and analyzes data on U.S. defense policy issues. His work focuses on the use of big data by the federal government, Iranian defense issues, and defense offsets and economic development. Prior to joining CSIS, he studied gun violence with the International Health & Epidemiology Research Center and helped establish nutritional and educational development projects with the Andean Alliance for Sustainable Development in Peru. He holds an M.A. in international development from the Monterey Institute of International Studies and a B.A. in international relations and history from Boston University.

Rhys McCormick is a research assistant with the Defense-Industrial Initiatives Group at CSIS. His work focuses on federal services contracting and defense contracting trends. Earlier, he interned with the Abshire-Inamori Leadership Academy at CSIS and the Peacekeeping and Stability Operations Institute at the U.S. Army War College. He holds a B.S. in security and risk analysis from the Pennsylvania State University with a concentration in intelligence analysis and modeling.

www.ingramcontent.com/pod-product-compliance
Ingram Content Group UK Ltd.
Pitfield, Milton Keynes, MK11 3LW, UK
UKHW051418150926
475561UK00005B/225

9 781442 225275